Joseph Conrad

His Moral Vision

Other Books by George A. Panichas

Adventure in Consciousness:
The Meaning of D. H. Lawrence's Religious Quest (1964)

Epicurus (1967)

The Reverent Discipline:
Essays in Literary Criticism and Culture (1974)

The Burden of Vision: Dostoevsky's Spiritual Art (1977)

The Courage of Judgment:
Essays in Criticism, Culture, and Society (1982)

The Critic as Conservator:
Essays in Literature, Society, and Culture (1992)

The Critical Legacy of Irving Babbitt:
An Appreciation (1999)

Growing Wings to Overcome Gravity:
Criticism as the Pursuit of Virtue (1999)

Editor, with George R. Hibbard and Allan Rodway,
Renaissance and Modern Essays:
Presented to Vivian de Sola Pinto
in Celebration of His Seventieth Birthday (1966)

Editor, *Mansions of the Spirit:*
Essays in Literature and Religion (1967)

Editor, *Promise of Greatness: The War of 1914–1918* (1968)

Editor, *The Politics of Twentieth-Century Novelists* (1971)

Editor, *The Simone Weil Reader* (1977)

Editor, *Irving Babbitt: Representative Writings* (1981)

Editor, with Claes C. Ryn, *Irving Babbitt in Our Time* (1986)

Editor, *Modern Age:*
The First Twenty-Five Years. A Selection (1988)

Editor, *In Continuity: The Last Essays of Austin Warren* (1996)

Joseph Conrad

His Moral Vision

George A. Panichas

Mercer University Press
Macon, Georgia USA
2005

ISBN 0-86554-936-2 MUP/H677

Joseph Conrad: His Moral Vision

Printed in the United States of America
First edition, June 2005

The paper used in this publication meets the minimum requirements of American National Standard for Information Sciences—Permanence of Paper for Printed Library Materials, ANSI Z39.48-1984.

Library of Congress Cataloging-in-Publication Data

Panichas, George Andrew.
Joseph Conrad : his moral vision / George A. Panichas. — 1st ed.
p. cm.
Includes bibliographical references and index.
ISBN 0-86554-936-2 (hardback : alk. paper)
1. Conrad, Joseph, 1857–1924—Ethics. 2. Didactic fiction, English—History and criticism. 3. Moral conditions in literature. 4. Ethics in literature. I. Title.
PR6005.04Z784935 2005
823'.912—dc22

2005002536

Contents

To
Russell Kirk
1918–1994
Man of Letters, Inspiring Friend, Conservator-at-Arms

Preface

The present work, the result of intensive studying and teaching during the past several decades, seeks to interpret the moral aspects of Joseph Conrad's major fiction and to concentrate on selected novels which delineate aspects of his moral imagination. It will perhaps be said that here is yet another book on a modern writer much honored for his place in the great tradition of the English novel. The fact remains that, although it has been more than eighty years since Conrad's death in 1924, his achievement continues to kindle the interest of readers and critics alike, which also does say something about the enduring power of his creative vision.

There can be no doubt that Conrad's fiction retains both a classic standing and a profound relevance of meaning, even as its meaning defies any finality of meaning in a postmodern world that must now address anew and in necessarily changing circumstances Conrad's view of human existence. But precisely because Conrad believed that life has meaning did he devote a lifetime to his imaginative art. This devotion, which reflects the strength of his acceptances and his affirmations, is in essence the guiding spirit of his contribution to arts and letters. It testifies also to his mission as a novelist whose paramount concern was with human fate in the modern age. The urgency of this concern was what shaped his perception of the meaning of things, and of the lives of men and women struggling with the living universe in all of its natural power and its moral terror.

In the exercise of his craft, Conrad responded to the human spectacle that he saw around him, to its rhythms and fluctuations, its tragedies and triumphs, its unending lines of creation and destruction, of hope and despair. His rendered response to this "enigmatical spectacle," and what lies deep beneath it, gives spectacle its substance and its identity. By synthesizing the human spectacle with human character Conrad was able to create a poetry of insight and illumination, and a profound sympathy for all "common mortals" who "must endure the load of the gifts from Heaven: the curse of facts and the blessings of illusions, the bitterness of our wisdom and the deceptive consolation of our folly," as he expressed it in his first book, *Almayer's Folly* (1895).

Conrad's novels are in the end great meditations on "the condition of life." Or, to put it in another way, his fictive meditations revolve around the outer and the inner life of humankind in all of its vulnerability, what he himself describes as "the unappeasable ocean of human life." For Conrad the natural world, with its infinite wonder and mystery, forever unchanging and yet always changing, needs to be perceived in all of its tensions and power if one is to enter its inward terrain. This task, he insisted, is important to "the workman of art": "Let him mature the strength of his imagination amongst the things of this earth, which it is his business to cherish and to know. . . . " To be sure, this is an ambitious task, but Conrad is also careful to stipulate: "I think that all ambitions are lawful except those which climb upward on the miseries or credulities of mankind."

Ultimately his novels explore and make known what takes place when the physical and metaphysical regions of intellect and emotion intersect and interconnect. Within this palpitant process "in the tumultuous open streams of existence," the reader feels the throbbing and pulling of the moral agon, whether directly or indirectly, consciously or unconsciously. Conrad renders this process as a "moment of vision" with dramatic and narrative vigor and force of analysis. This is precisely what gives his novels their energy, their dynamic, their urgency, and their unique resonance. As such, Conrad's creative achievement is one that inexorably enlarges "the general experience of mankind."

This book is not simply a critical or academic exercise that revolves around the adjudication of an artist's vision or that strives to scrutinize and measure it in relation to other writers and their works. Proving to a reader the merits of a novelist's works is not the goal here. That excellent purpose has been convincingly done by any number of gifted critics on an international scale. Rather it is my primary intention to interpret the endless riches of Conrad's visionary power as a novelist, to expand and to deepen a reader's understanding of his major fiction as it has been critically acclaimed. The basic and impelling purpose here, then, is that of exploring the extremities of Conrad's vision and of grasping its depth of meaning, its subtleties of text and context. The job of interpretation, clearly, has no set boundary if the stuff of imagination has unconfined value.

The office of the interpreter, in complementing and augmenting the office of the critic, endeavors above all to explain the meaning of text and texture, and in turn to quicken the artist's language and meaning, by variously re-creating the artist's vision to its ultimate point of application. If the function of criticism serves to fulfill the demands of judgment and valuation, the function of interpretation is an ascending one in the comprehension of life and the universe. Without criticism we have no literary bearings or general principles of order; with interpretation we experience, intuitively and dramatically, a work of literature, we enter its deeper consciousness, what takes place in it, what its significations confront us with, what private responses it engenders in us, in short, what literary discourse it finally produces once we travel the pathways of the creative process. Interpretation thus heightens one's inner experience of imaginative art; it assists one to see things not seen before, to infiltrate and explore the regions of language and meaning, and, finally, to illuminate their revelations.

Criticism, in the old sense, and careful interpretation, in the humanistic tradition, are not exclusive pursuits but, as this book attempts to show, a mutually necessary process, each needing the other, each illumining the other, with both attaining a tertiary function: elucidating words in the text; sharpening the reader's appreciation of the writer's vision; and approaching the text's moral meaning with reverence. The synthesis, or attunement, of criticism and interpretation is, then, the driving force of the exposition and commentation found in the discussion of Conrad's novels and meaning. However, this synthesis must not be viewed as a species of system building. As the philosophical thinker Eric Voegelin has reminded us, the construction of a system is often antecedent to the disordering falsification of human and moral reality.

Much of postmodernist literary theory during recent decades, especially dominant in the academy, has exerted a reductivist orientation that leads to the erosion of language and literature. The synthesis I designate above attempts to countermand the hubristic *litterateurs* who would gladly erase the "dignity of man" and, concomitantly, the dignity of literature. Postmodernist literary study has turned its back precisely on the spirit of synthesis that inheres in the approaches and aims of this book. In a sense, then, this book strives to restore the old humanist tools of criticism that enable one to transcend the relativistic and ideological productions devised by many of today's intellectuals and technicians who reject the spiritual components of culture and character. Clearly we moved from a state of dehumanization to one of decadence in the course of the twentieth century, and increasingly we suffer the full consequences in the twin realms of the imagination and of the critical pursuit. In short, we have retreated from a metaphysics of art to an ideology of art, even as the art of fiction and the art of criticism transform radically into a deconstructive project.

Though Conrad stressed that he neither nurtured a didactic purpose nor put on a novel "any particular moral complexion," he was careful to add that "every subject in the region of intellect and emotion must have a morality of its own if it is treated at all sincerely." Indeed, "even the most artful of writers," he was to admit, "will give himself (and his morality) away in about every third sentence." In his writings, he goes on to state, the "varied shades of moral significance . . . are very numerous." It is precisely the interpretation of these "varied shades of moral significance" that is at the core of this study, which seeks to stay within the discrete range of Conrad's "vision of things" when, as he points out, "I cannot sufficiently insist upon the truth that when I sit down to write my intentions are always blameless however deplorable the ultimate effect of the act may turn out to be."

Honoring these "intentions" constitutes for the author of this study a reverent discipline that dictates sharing a moral honesty with a creative genius like Conrad who depicts the rhythms of the moral sense that play a pivotal role in the realms of his imagination. Conrad, it can be said, possesses and celebrates the moral sense, or feeling, as a principle of discrimination that emerges from an intuitive perception of the interrelatedness of man and the circumnambient universe, to employ here D. H. Lawrence's phraseology from his lively essay "Art and Morality," which appeared in 1925. This relation, he avowed, has a fourth-dimensional quality; and morality in the novel is the "humbling and changing *balance*."

In his novels Conrad reveals what Lawrence calls "things in their different relationships," within whose vibrancies and tremulations we get momentaneous glimpses of temporal life and eternity itself. Conrad's moral sense defines his contemplation of things, values, people; it impels his aspiration as a novelist who proposes to express and objectify "the condition of art" to which he aspires and on the basis of which he makes his distinctive "appeal." This sentence from Conrad's preface to *The Nigger of the "Narcissus"* (1897) contains perhaps the clearest expression of his creed as a "workman of art," and of the indwelling moral impulse and justification that enjoin its exposition: "And art itself may be defined as a single-minded attempt to render the highest kind of justice to the visible universe, by bringing to light the truth, manifold and one, underlying its every aspect."

In its parts and in its whole this book focuses steadfastly on Conrad's moral vision and how he renders and communicates its attributes. Such a vision is implicitly intuitive and inclusive insofar as it relates to the novelist's view of the totality of human existence, a view that surges beyond what is simply immediate or transient and that accents the writer's apprehension of general truths and values. In a Conradian novel we find the enactment of a particular moral problem in theme and technique. Thus at the center of Conrad's vision, it can be asserted, is an overarching moral preoccupation, which the chapters in this book seek to signal and illuminate. The force and the continuity of this moral preoccupation are its evident, if not its premier, signs when one considers the corpus of Conrad's writings and the background of their creation.

Conrad's supreme capacity as a novelist is to involve his reader in confronting acutely moral questions; and he is especially adroit not only in catching the strains and paradoxes that accrue in the aesthetic process, but also in compelling the reader to engage them in an artistic "transaction." Conrad himself is entirely clear regarding his mission as a novelist: to make his reader apprehend the stuff of his vision, to find in it the special energies and pattern of existence that are an organic phase of the narrative action as it unfolds, ramifies, and impacts, and to derive from it confluent lessons of human existence that have individual and universal appeal. In such a process, the novelist refurbishes reality in forms addressed to new (and yet old) needs. The novelist V. S. Naipaul points to the protean value of Conrad's imagination in its origins and end in these words: "In fiction he did not seek to discover; he sought to explain; the discovery of every tale . . . is a moral one." Naipaul's observation has an added relevance in reckoning the literary value of interpretation in the study of Conrad's fiction, to which this book proposes to make a contribution.

Moral darkness and warfare are quintessential elements that enshroud the world of Conrad's fiction. His men and women are often drawn as prisoners of this darkness, but also as strugglers trying to live their lives in the world in which they happen to be, the world into which they have been thrown. Within this darkness, in a limit-situation that remains impervious to their inner yearnings, his heroes and heroines quest for self-meaning. Finding themselves and identifying their character, those unique qualities that best mark them and distinguish them from others, is their destined task, which they must toil to attain, often against strange and inexplicable resistance, natural and human. Their toils are demanding, exhausting, at times mystifying, as they strive to come to terms with their predicament, or at least to recognize the difficulties of their efforts. Sometimes these efforts end in defeat or in impasse or in death; and even their advances and victories emerge from the costliest of efforts.

Moral absolutes are generally elusive or arrested by unknown, indefinable, baffling forces that suddenly spring up to bar the way or to blur the value of any definitive gain. Darkness and variance tend to intervene in ways that are hard to untangle and to contain. How does one grasp moral certitude from the jaws of an immoral phenomenon or force or exigency? This question must be faced again and again by Conrad's people trying to comprehend destiny. His men and women are often in pursuit of some viable form of spiritual succor in a universe that makes that higher quest both vulnerable and problematic. This is why, too, moral darkness and moral strife have such enormous ardor and why they also heighten the conditions and circumstances of warfare, visible and invisible. Conrad's contemplation of the forms and modes of this consuming struggle is what, in the end, gives to his art a dynamic proportion as he renders its inflictions in their totality.

Clearly Conrad's great novels effect in us moral shock and awaken us to both human and universal values that too often tend to be hidden or unheeded. If Conrad does not manifest an explicitly religious imagination, as does a Dante or a Dostoevsky, he does uncover moral and eternal verities insofar as he ventures beyond the temporal veil in his exploration of the interiors of existence. Invariably he relates, as only true creative genius can, a sense of gravity—permanent truths when the state of the soul is at great risk. Or, to put it in another way, Conrad is attuned to the moral constant, which he intuits in its changing reality and in its transcendence. Indeed, he makes the moral constant more real in both its experiential and existential substances, which he integrates in his art in their symbolic power and moral gradations.

When one looks at Conrad's men and women one perceives these gradations in their ebb and flow, their failure and triumph, their exertion and regression. Some of his characters are at a terminal point of inertia, when their moral energy is immobilized; when they are depleted of any moral feeling—emptied of the moral sense, except their self-abandonment, boredom, abnegation, in short, the malaise of soul that makes them immune to any moral claim or reminder. Conrad does not concentrate so much on moral dichotomies as much as he does on moral dissonances that affect his characters in various degrees of intensity, complexity, sensation.

He discloses to the reader certain elementary moral revelations that capture human experience in its myriad hues and colors. His art, his vision, in fine, is astonishingly free of any ideological twisting of reality in order to accommodate some dialectical system. The human world and human nature, in Conrad's novels, are evoked in all of their variation. His art emerges from his disinterested vision of order and disorder that contains within it vicissitudes of inner and outer tumult in their nakedness and impingement. He neither harbors nor surrenders to romantic illusions; unrelentingly, he portrays the antinomies, caprices, and speciousness that inflame our human timber.

Yet however bleak or grim his fictional universe, however desperate the actions of his characters, however fearsome and beguiling their predicament, Conrad's moral vision is never compromised or shaken. His evocation of human isolation, skepticism, solitariness, and betrayal can be unassuaging in its intensity. As he memorably acknowledges in one of his letters, the world is like "a knitting machine," it "knits us in" and "knits us out"; it is one in which "there is no morality, no knowledge and no hope." In this connection, the novelist E. M. Forster singles out Conrad for criticism in the course of a review of the latter's *Notes on Life and Letters* (1921): "He does not respect all humanity. . . . He will not despise men, yet cannot respect them, and consequently our careers seem to him important and unimportant at the same time, and our fates . . . 'poignant, intensely interesting, and not of the slightest consequence.' " This often-repeated, facile censure of Conrad is one that the present book seeks to correct, or at least to demonstrate its inadequacy, even its fallacy.

Conrad's vision of human existence is a planetary and not an epistemological one; it is tied to the realities of place and people, of nature and life; to the moral real in its multifarious modes; to good and evil elements as these invariably clash or congeal. His is not the sophistic view of, say, an indiscriminating optimist or pessimist, but of entities of consciousness as these circumscribe the human equation. Nor should we expect from Conrad some astringent statement of principles of behavior though he is intuitively aware of life-principles and life-values that can be identified in aesthetic and moral phenomena.

His imaginative art cannot simply or finally be reduced to morality, but is irrevocably attached to moral forms, which he apprehends intuitively and symbolically. In Conrad we encounter the moral imagination as he transforms and integrates it in art-speech, and not according to moral fiat, classification, or catalogue; critics who ignore this, who demand from Conrad moral and philosophical objectification or methodology, fail to enter the world of his creative expression. This is a world that the chapters in this book, individually and collectively, want to open up to the reader.

In one very important sense Conrad's novels generate a creative process that a reader takes part in as a moral dynamic and a moral crisis. The origin and the development of this crisis, in its tensive vibrations, testify to the underlying power of Conrad's vision, which this book seeks to assay. To interpret this cumulative process, in its constituents and its consequences, is a salient aim of each chapter as it addresses the crisis, or crises, a reader undergoes in the particular novel being focused on in its aesthetic forms and discriminations.

Conrad's fiction can in fact be read as a succession of individuating moral crises, each entailing moral recognition of human experience and meaning. This moral crisis, in its astonishing immediacy, is not to be seen as a quest for religious faith, but rather as the reenergizing of the moral sense that Conrad helps us to perceive more fully: to experience not only its perils and terrors, in their uttermost constraints, but also its discoveries in sight of moral recovery, in short, attaining "awareness of the possibilities of life," to borrow here F. R. Leavis's phrase.

This book proposes to reclaim and reactivate the moral essences of art, exclusive of a philosophy of morality. These moral essences, alas, are mostly dismissed or scorned by contemporary literary theorists and practitioners. Hence, meticulous attention to Conrad's language must be duly paid if one is to grasp the creative expression of his meaning. The power of the word, of the language of his imagination, is preeminent in any interpretive study of his prose and fiction, and it accounts, too, for the frequent employment of Conrad's own words, as well as for the conveyance of the moral perspectives which his text gives rise to and from which the interpretations of these perspectives are derived.

It should be iterated that the chapters, or more correctly the individual essays, in this book are not organized and arranged according to strictly chronological or thematic principles of development. Rather they attempt to deepen and enlarge and enrich the reader's perceptualization of Conrad's moral cosmos in its variegating components, in both its vertical and horizontal lines as these take on sensual forms in their myriad interconnections. These lines are mirrored by the technical properties of Conrad's craft of fiction. Within these lines, contiguous or not, we apprehend Conrad's moral landscape, we delve into its remotest regions, we experience its mystery, intricacy, ambiguity. In the end we also envision its total meaning, as it becomes progressively accessible to revelation and understanding.

Clearly, Conrad's moral landscape offers us glimpses of concrete actions that can lead to levels of moral enlightenment. These actions, Conrad shows, are not necessarily salvific in scope, but they do dramatize the human condition as it translates into expression. Nor does Conrad stipulate a moral imperative, judgment, sui generis; rather, he registers a moral potency that awaits assimilation on the part of the reader, who is privy to what that potency entails. Mining and discerning this moral potency in all of its oscillations and turbulences is an organic part of this study, which in effect moves beyond specific critical criteria to land on the side of the metaphysical.

Conrad's moral vision has to be comprehended in its spatial and temporal qualities as these metamorphose into human nature and human experience. His aesthetic process does not assert concepts but creates them visually and experientially. Conrad's fiction in this respect magnifies the moral sense, which is all too often dormant, and awakens the moral consciousness according to the degree to which one's sense-perceptions are vivified. The novels under discussion here illustrate how Conrad's aesthetic process radiates his impressions of reality—impressions that are as poetic and meditative as they are presaging. Implicit in these impressions is the high density of decisions and acts that spell out the moral fate of Conrad's men and women.

In a letter dated June 26, 1902, Henry James wrote these words about Conrad: "*Do* let me recommend him to you in the name of his charming, conscientious, uncommon work. It has truly a kind of disinterested independent nobleness." This interpretive study echoes and enlarges upon James's recommendation from an intrinsically moral outlook. Because Conrad's moral vision is inexhaustible in value and relevance, it requires new and plentiful interpretation if his meaning to us is to be acknowledged. The ramifications and the essences of Conrad's moral imagination are unending in their significance to us, as this study endeavors to confirm. And it has yet to be appreciated for its beneficences. Our inveterate preoccupations with the imagination in its diabolic and subhuman forms cannot be allowed to overrule or to excise those confluent areas of humane concern and moral significance that Conrad proffers in civilizing ways to his readers.

In Conrad's novels, in his moral vision, there are distant realms of meaning that are eminently reachable. It is not a matter of pinning down some meaning by making it absolute and inviolable, for this in itself goes against the spirit of interpretation, the largesse and the generosity of which can offer genuine insights that are rewarding to a reader searching for a more complete understanding of a work of art. Literary interpretation is at its maximum free of dogma, aspiring as it does for the kind of freedom that goes hand-in-hand with responsibility. Such an alliance is rooted in balance and sympathy, qualities that are indispensable if the literary interpreter is to succeed in his function; if, that is, he is to help a reader assess an artist's vision in ways hitherto unknown or untouched or simply overlooked.

How does one mediate between a reader and a work of art? How does one foster dialogue between the reader and the artist? These are questions that the literary interpreter keeps in mind when looking at the text and attempting to broaden the reader's response to it. In this respect, interpretations are ultimately forms of encouragement that can light the reader's way through the text and enable him to see and to tie things together in a more coherent and unified pattern. Humanistic expectations underlie these intentions, and hopes, for the cause of the *litterae humaniores*. No cause could be higher, or consequences more important, for the interpreter.

The preceding prefatory reflections constitute a plea for the humane values of interpretation as a useful literary and critical tool in elucidating fictive texts. In especial these are reflections designed to clarify the operative structure and ethos of an interpretive study of Conrad's major novels. There is no need here to apologize for the particular approach chosen to examine his fiction and to search in it for the different levels of meaning it contains. The content, and specifically the moral content, is so rich and challenging that it calls for making every possible effort to probe its total thrust.

Clarity and enlargement of understanding is a literary aim that cannot be reduced in quality and value, whatever zealous literary ideologues enclosed in their private laboratories may otherwise claim. This book strives to speak to the reader and not to the constructors of an agenda. The contexts of the interpretations offered here belong to the larger context of a humane civilization. To insist on this point is necessary if the faculty of interpretation is to be rescued from those critical practitioners who have extra- and nonliterary ends in mind, and who unilaterally dispense with the reader and with the creative artist in order to chase after their presuppositions—and solipsisms. Steering clear of these ambitions, or schemes, is an implicit task of this book.

The arduous wrestlings of soul, in concert with social anguish, are unending and consuming. The drama of the human soul in conflict with itself and with the world is a dynamic one; in this drama, as it unravels, the self encounters its self in other selves as portrayed by Conrad. Even as one escapes from the world, one meets the world again and again; gravity and grace are ever in contention in such a world, and there is no safe sanctuary for anyone except when in the grip of illusion. The voices we hear speaking echo this contention: its fear, violence, perfidy. Feelings of helplessness, disenchantment, ambiguity flow back and forth in an unpredictable and frightening pattern of emotion and thought.

Physical death and moral death fuse in Conrad's narratives in ways that disclose the vagaries of the state of the soul both in its historical and societal, and in its personal and spiritual transfigurations. This dimension of Conrad's art comes under special focus in the development of the interpretations of the novels discussed here. The autonomy of each novel is revered so as to ascertain and interpret its moral locale and place it in the geography of Conrad's moral imagination.

Moral effort and recovery, which also embody intrinsic possibilities of human life, are in the final analysis requisite components of reconciliation in Conrad's work. Courage and endurance are virtues that he salutes in human life. Certainly, Conrad's writings go directly to the heart of the crisis of modernity, of an abandoned world "reduced to the condition of things," when, in Samuel Beckett's words, "man can only despair of hope, can only not wait or wait." But Conrad's incipiently tragic vision is redeemed by his affirmation of old verities and, in his own words, "a few very simple ideas . . . as old as the hills." Humility is the final word in the lexicon of his ethos. To slight humility as a sacred principle is to consign Conrad's visionary power to the "heart of darkness," a perpetual prison house. If anything, Conrad's fiction consistently affirms possibilities of transcendence when they are enacted by an abiding sense of responsibility, honor, fidelity.

The study of literature can have no educational authority if an endless craving to go "beyond criticism" and "beyond interpretation" in effect goes beyond the language of the artist's vision. The rage for order thus turns into a rage for disorder as the *logos* is annexed by the forces of abstraction. This book seeks to deter a surrender to such forces and to the abnormalities and aberrations they seek to enjoin as new and cruel paradigms. These are the larger considerations that guide this book and that mold its spirit of interpretation. Above all, there is its tacit belief that readers are not to be treated as captives of extremist literary theory.

"I will preface no longer, but proceed," the seventeenth-century English writer and biographer Izaak Walton rightly asserts. The principal part of this book now awaits the reader's inspection, as it proceeds to sustain and illustrate the reasons for and intent of this study. The hope is that this book will facilitate a reader's journey into Conrad's world, therein to discover areas of his moral imagination perhaps not distinguished before, or hardly considered, or just barely noticed. Within Conrad's world, then, this study strives to demonstrate how moral discriminations develop and evolve in the human consciousness; how they mirror character and conduct; how the human world is to be seen; how human fate is to be met and borne.

This book bids the reader to embark on travels to the country of Joseph Conrad's moral imagination. If the book's interpretations help the reader not only to appreciate the novelist's craft and meaning, but also to absorb his humane insights and sympathies, then even the most modest of its expectations will have been realized.

A Note on the Text

Chapters 1, 3, 4, and 5 were originally published in *Modern Age: A Quarterly Review*, as follows: "Joseph Conrad's *The Secret Agent* as a Moral Tale" (Spring 1997): 143-52; "Moral Warfare in Joseph Conrad's *Victory*" (Summer 1999): 239-50; "The Powers of Moral Darkness in Joseph Conrad's *Nostromo*" (Spring 2002): 129-46; "Joseph Conrad's *Under Western Eyes: In Sight of Moral Discovery*" (Fall 1998): 359-73.

Chapter 2 first appeared under the title "The Moral Sense in Joseph Conrad's *Lord Jim*," in *Humanitas* 13/1 (2000): 10-30.

Chapter 6 (*Chance*) and 7 (*The Rover*) are printed here for the first time.

Chapter 1

The Secret Agent

I

Russell Kirk recalls that as a youth he had purchased in Lansing, Michigan, with his month's allowance, a half set of the works of Joseph Conrad (1857–1924). Later, in his early twenties, while serving in the military, he happened to come across, in Salt Lake City, Utah, the missing half of that broken set, and acquired it out of his private's pay. His appreciation of Conrad's writings endured to the end of his life. In 1993, when his *Politics of Prudence* was published, Kirk returned to Conrad for a parting salute to a novelist who has exceptional appeal to readers interested in the literature of politics.[1]

In calling attention to Conrad's importance, Kirk must also have had in mind those higher values and virtues he ascribed to the moral imagination, which for Kirk aspires "to the apprehending of right order in the soul and right order in the commonwealth."[2] Utilizing the power of the word and the requisite imaginative responsibility, the artist can play an active role in orienting a reader toward something higher, in growing wings to overcome gravity, as Plato expresses it. The artist, in short, has the capacity to fulfill the function of visionaries who also can serve as shepherds of the peoples. The artist's impact can thus contain both a moral and a redemptive element. It is precisely in this sense that Conrad's greatest novels engage the reader in the moral life; and "hold truth enough," as Conrad's narrator in *Under Western Eyes* (1911) observes, "to help the moral discovery which should be the object of every tale." Yet moral discovery is never detached from the moral reality which Conrad unceasingly confronts and which he recreates with astonishing intensity as he takes the reader into "the heart of darkness" and all of its perils. In Conrad's fiction, moral discovery must ultimately emerge from moral reality in the extended form of moral courage. This triple process constitutes what one critic calls "the morality of Conrad's

---

[1](Bryn Mawr PA, 1993) 73.

[2]*Eliot and His Age: T. S. Eliot's Moral Imagination in the Twentieth Century* (New York, 1971) 7-8.

imagination." "At the center of vision, then, Conrad locates a profound and desperate opposition between disintegration and the creative engagement stirred to life in his reader."[3] So writes Daniel Melnick in words that further clarify the nature of Conrad's moral imagination, what it is and does, what it leads to and results in.

Conrad's novel *The Secret Agent* (1907) particularly illustrates not only his moral universality but also his moral indictment of the betrayal of order, which a civilized society needs for its existence. His view of "the natural sensibilities of mankind" in this novel, in the context of what he calls "the moral squalor of the tale," is unyielding in "its unsparing indignation and underlying pity," as Conrad wrote in his "Author's Note," published later, in 1920, which pinpoints his aims in writing *The Secret Agent*. Perhaps no other of his novels better confirms George Orwell's assertion that Conrad's most memorable passages and scenes deal with the sea, but that his most mature insights emerge "when he touches dry land."[4]

The Secret Agent records the disintegration, with all the manifold consequences, of both the human community and the human soul. The "personages" who live and move, darkly and sinisterly, in this "monstrous town," variously typify the "revolutionary spirit" that possesses and transforms them into "the devils" of F. M. Dostoevsky's 1873 novel by that name. No less than the Russian novelist, Conrad has no sympathy for anarchists, applying to them an "ironic method," in "the earnest belief that ironic treatment alone would enable me to say all I felt I would have to say in scorn as well as in pity," as he wrote in his note. In relating the story "to its anarchistic end of utter desolation, madness and despair," he goes on to say, "I have not intended to commit gratuitous outrage on the feelings of mankind." At the heart of Conrad's imaginative genius is the impersonalizing intelligence, the disinterestedness, that gives to his fiction its ability to record what "is fundamental, what is enduring and essential," as Conrad wrote in the preface to *The Nigger of the "Narcissus"* (1897), and "by the power of the written word, to make you hear, to make you feel—it is, before all to make you *see*."

---

[3]"The Morality of Conrad's Imagination: *Heart of Darkness* and *Nostromo*," in *Modern Critical Views: Joseph Conrad*, edited and with an introduction by Harold Bloom (New York, 1986) 117.

[4]*The Collected Essays, Journalism and Letters of George Orwell*, vol. 3, *As I Please, 1943–1945*, ed. Sonia Orwell and Ian Angus (New York, 1986) 389.

The Secret Agent evokes the dramatic range and depth of Conrad's moral concerns. A novel of rigorous moral exploration, it forces one to see the things of the world that one has hitherto not seen, or has refused to see, or has feared to see. As such this novel also helps a reader to gain some semblance of "moral discovery" and in the process to discern more sharply the deeper meanings of life viewed in the context of assertions that have a confluent and recurrent motif in *The Secret Agent*: "This ain't an easy world"; "life doesn't stand much looking into"; "it may be good for one not to know too much." Conrad's "ironic method" is a dominant and even a personal aspect of this novel; his use of irony becomes, in Thomas Mann's phrase, "a form of morality." The ironic method employed in *The Secret Agent* serves as a contradictory outcome of the novel's happenings—the conscious failure of the novel's men and women to avoid confronting the hard facts of existence, or as Conrad writes: "They refrained from going to the bottom of facts and motives." *The Secret Agent* shows, inexorably, a profound contrast between man and his hopes, fears, wishes, and undertakings and a dark, inflexible fate. Or to put it in another way, Conrad's ironic treatment attains his special aim to dislodge the illusions of those who, avoiding or disregarding the data of human existence, embrace false or safe conceptions, and remain transfixed in the gulf between appearance and reality. The moral momentum and gravity of this novel are to be observed in the stripping away of cherished illusions. Moral discovery triumphs in this process.

The world we encounter in this novel, set in London in the winter and spring of 1886, is draped in shadows and grime, which Conrad likens to a "descent into a slimy aquarium." The first chapter of *The Secret Agent* puts us in contact immediately with a sordid world and people. What we see here and those we meet embody what is morally slothful, evidenced early on in the appearance of Adolf Verloc, shop-owner in Soho and *agent provocateur*: "His eyes were naturally heavy; he had an air of having wallowed, fully dressed, all day on an unmade bed." Indolence and idleness seem to shroud his persona, "undemonstrative and burly in a fat-pig style." Even the streets he walks, in pursuit of his devious political purposes, bring into relief Verloc's inner and outer condition. Here, in the midst of "London's topographical mysteries," Verloc has come to a foreign embassy, which employs him as a secret operative, to meet Privy Councillor Wurmt, Chancelier d'Ambassade, whose own weary and melancholy presence heightens the purpose of this meeting of two men harboring a purely destructive aim to create social disorder: "the occurrence of something definite which should stimulate their [the police's] vigilance"; "the accentuation of the unrest" through a "series of outrages." Immediately following this initial phase of the meeting, Verloc is then taken to the private room of Mr. Vladimir, First Secretary, a smooth and witty favorite in society circles, who quietly but firmly centers on the type of dynamite outrage Verloc is to perpetrate with the help of other anarchists-terrorists: blowing up Greenwich Observatory, "of the first meridian." The foreign official, Russian no doubt, believes that such an outrage would push England to adopt sterner political measures of suppression of political crimes: "This country," he insists, "is absurd with its sentimental regard for individual liberty. . . . "

The Secret Agent portrays no single, genuine hero, concentrating instead on a grouping, mostly anarchists, of characters. Conrad's portrayal throughout is steadfast in its objectivity as he seeks to focus on men and women as "shams," without principles and without any loyalty to first principles; and throughout the focus is on moral breakdown, its features and consequences. The novel has, in effect, a parabolic thrust that helps one see through the anarchists in their repulsiveness and degeneracy; indeed, their slothfulness is always magnified, with graphic emphasis on physical extremes, as in the case of Michaelis, "the ticket-of-leave apostle," "with an enormous stomach," as well as in the case of Verloc himself, whose face and figure disclose a "fat-pig style": "He's fat—the animal," Mr. Vladimir thinks to himself during their meeting. They lack precisely that discipline, inner and outer, that society requires if it is to rise above a protoplasmic state.

The discerning moral faculty, as Conrad believed and showed, enables one to discriminate judgmentally between qualities of existence, thought, and character, to distinguish between vice and virtue. *The Secret Agent* depicts both the absence and the entailing costs of this faculty. From a moral angle, *The Secret Agent* is the most fearless of Conrad's novels; his controlled contempt for the anarchists, and for moral lethargy and indifference, is undeviating. Invariably the novelist's moral responsibility is on display. No doubt T. S. Eliot had this dynamic in mind when insisting that Conrad (along with Hawthorne and Dostoevsky) possesses and enacts the "essential moral preoccupation. . . . Evil is rare, bad is common. Evil cannot even be perceived but by a very few."[5] *The Secret Agent* has both a

---

[5]F. O. Matthiessen, *The Achievement of T. S. Eliot: An Essay on the Nature of*

ferocity and a momentum of vision in its exposure of agents of moral laceration. Its "dark vision of megalopolis," of London, goes hand-in-hand with its dark vision of moral and spiritual inertia, of stagnancy, with the horrors of which Conrad confronts the reader, who is pressed by Conrad to enlist a profound moral effort in detecting and gauging the horrors. *The Secret Agent*, in many respects, becomes a kind of catechetical novel, that is, one of moral education.

II

For Conrad the anarchists, who are among the main figures in his novel and whom we first find gathered in the parlor of Verloc's house, personify moral corruption and negation. Whether Conrad is viewing Michaelis, "the ticket-of-leave apostle of humanitarian hopes," or Karl Yundt, the old terrorist, or Comrade Alexander Ossipon, the principal writer of revolutionary leaflets, he depicts them as odious human beings, ugly and malevolent in both their demeanor and their abstract discussions, which blend fully with London and its "enormity of cold, black, wet, muddy, inhospitable accumulation of bricks, slates, and stones, things in themselves unlovely and unfriendly to man." From them we can expect nothing of substance or meaning; their common language is one of personal, social, and moral rot. They have no reverence for moral value or for the virtue of loyalty that Conrad reveres. Their world is an abyss of negations, without acceptance or affirmation or any possibility of growth or ascent. Circumvention and circuitousness are its main reference points. It is Stevie, the half-witted brother of Winnie, Verloc's wife, who provides here the image of the world of the anarchists. While seated quietly at a deal table, in the kitchen adjacent to the parlor where the anarchists are meeting, he is to be seen "drawing circles, circles, circles; innumerable circles . . . a coruscating whirl of circles . . . suggesting . . . cosmic chaos. . . . " *The Secret Agent* reveals the chaos in life that honors no value, no principle, no virtue, no tradition. And the anarchists are breeders of chaos, of "that old confusion, which we call chaos, wherein without order, without fashion, confusedly lay the discordant seeds of things," to recall here an old definition.[6]

Poetry (London and New York, 1958) 24.

[6]See the second definition of "Chaos" in *The Oxford English Dictionary*, vol. 2, ed. J. A. H. Murray et al. (Oxford UK, 1933; repr. 1961) 173.

The Secret Agent is a collective symbol of chaos. Both the revolutionists and the legal and political authorities respect no central value or discipline. They are "hollow men" who exert no moral effort or judgment, preferring to drift in the world. In all matters, their minds and bearing seem to go in circles. Indeed, once the attempted bombing of the Observatory takes place, when Stevie, delegated by Verloc as the carrier of the bomb, trips and is blown to pieces, the Assistant Commissioner of Police, and head of the Special Crimes Department, shows no appreciation of his renowned subordinate, Chief Inspector Heat, in tracking down the culprits—"his appreciation . . . excluded all notion of moral confidence." Human interrelations and discourse throughout lack sincerity at all levels, even as there is a common refusal to address the nexus of cause and effects. Chief Inspector Heat actually uses Secret Agent Verloc by providing him with police protection in exchange for information regarding revolutionaries, their networks, plans, and activities. Moral integrity is an unaffordable luxury, as Conrad brings out in these words spoken by the Chief Inspector to his superior: "I must do my work in my own way. . . . When it comes to that I would deal with the devil himself, and take the consequences. These are things not fit for everybody to know."

From top to bottom people personify secrecy. The "great Personage," Sir Ethelred, who holds political power, meets with the Assistant Commissioner concerning the bomb outrage, and stresses, "Don't go into details. I have no time for that. . . . Spare me the details." (In this respect, he is not different from Winnie Verloc, whose "philosophy consisted in not taking notice of the inside of facts.") Moral responsibility and moral action require effort of attention and decision, and in *The Secret Agent* these needs are shunned. Conrad shows us the profound costs of such shunning in the light of fear, apathy, indifference, expediency. And here Conrad addresses the human situation, even as he answers those who pursue the comfort of illusions. Sir Ethelred discloses the political dimension of moral laxity; political leadership, Conrad seems to be saying, can be notoriously shallow and insincere. The Assistant Commissioner, of course, seeks help from "The Personage" in restraining Chief Inspector Heat from protecting a double agent like Verloc. Such protection, he reports, leads to "some species of authorized scoundrelism" blatantly ignoring "the work of anarchism." He seeks, and receives, permission to investigate the circumstances of the bomb-outrage personally, knowing as he does that the address on Stevie's clothing, "the only piece of material evidence" discovered and reported by Heat, may lead him to the bottom of the affair.

The Assistant Commissioner thereupon proceeds to go to Mr. Verloc's shop, at 32 Brett Street, "sullen, brooding, and sinister."

Conrad's image of the descent into a subterranean world is vividly rendered in his detailed portrayal, at the very middle of the novel, of Mrs. Verloc's mother when she moves to an almshouse. Determined not to burden her daughter and Verloc any longer, and hoping above all that her removal would insure her son Stevie's place in living with his devoted sister, the mother leaves Brett Street. This harrowing journey is likened to a journey in a "Cab of Death,"—"Crawling behind an infirm horse . . . on wobbly wheels and with a maimed driver on the box," all this taking place at "Night, the early dirty night, the sinister, noisy, hopeless, and rowdy night of South London." This grim journey enters a realm in which, as the mother reflects, "everything decays, wears out . . . the rule of decay affecting all things human and some things divine." The entire scene, which Conrad evokes in a language of pathos, further accentuates the absence of light in a novel in which everything is suffused in murky shadows and in eerie circumstances afflicting life and soul. Conrad's men and women "dwell in the thick of darkness" to recall here a biblical image of "the power of darkness." "It was a bad world. Bad! Bad!" exclaims an agitated Stevie at one point as he contemplates intuitively the scene of "human and equine misery" once the removal to the almshouse has been completed. In the meantime, "the smell of fried fish" permeates the scene and atmosphere—the street like "a slimy aquarium from which the water had been run off."

In the novel's total situation moral darkness torments both man's inner and outer worlds, both body and soul. The men who drift or wallow in this darkness by refusing "not to know too much," who refuse, that is to say, to make any moral effort, all thus choose to live in a moral and spiritual vacuum. Conrad, it is interesting to note, dedicated *The Secret Agent* as "this simple tale of the XIX century" to H. G. Wells. It would be more correct to call it a moral tale in which the novelist portrays the results of moral affliction and of life that has no moral center or worth. The refrain "Put out the light, and then put out the light" is heard again and again in the novel. Indeed, the only character in the novel at all aware of impoverishing moral and social conditions is an utterly helpless and expendable Stevie: "You could do anything with that boy, Adolf. . . . He would go through fire for you," Mrs. Verloc exclaims to her husband. Dialogue in the novel, one is often reminded, is muffled, joyless, cruelly detached, a slave of secrecy.

Its primary aim is that of always avoiding the reality of truth—"disinclined to look under the surface of things," as Conrad writes.

Any revelation of truth emerges with difficulty, circuitously, as when Chief Inspector Heat, relieved of the case of the bomb outrage, arrives one evening at the "shop of shoddy wares" with the express purpose of speaking privately to an absent Verloc. It is on this particular occasion that Mrs. Verloc gradually learns the news of Stevie's death in Greenwich, unreported by her husband, who seemed to be guarding the incident with the kind of secretiveness appropriate to his work. Heat now shows her, and Winnie identifies, the label sewn on the inside of Stevie's coat with the Brett Street address written in marking ink. Verloc's return to the shop at exactly this point adds to the suspense and fatefulness of the revelation. The two men go into the parlor to discuss matters, as a startled and aroused Mrs. Verloc listens to their conversation through the door's keyhole. Now she "heard nothing but murmurs, whose mysteriousness was less nightmarish to her brain than the horrible suggestions of shaped words. . . . Mrs. Verloc pressed her ear to the keyhole; her lips were blue, her hands cold as ice, and her pale face, in which the two eyes seemed like two black holes, felt to her as if it were enveloped in flames."

For Winnie, truth, no less than life, *ain't easy*, she having to recognize the cruel and irreducible fact that her husband had enlisted Stevie to carry the bomb in the attempt to blow up Greenwich Observatory, the task delegated to Verloc by Mr. Vladimir. The intense "agitation of rage and despair" fixed her pose into one of "perfect immobility." One realizes, too, that Winnie's sole reason for marrying Verloc, in the first place, was her belief that he would be a devoted guardian of Stevie. But Stevie, of course, carrying a detonator supplied by the Little Professor, had stumbled against the root of a tree and fell, "blown to fragments in a state of innocence and in the conviction of being engaged in a humanitarian enterprise." Winnie's habit of not taking notice of the inside of facts has now been equally sundered, even as her notion of marital stability has been destroyed. She now experiences not only the death of a brother but also the death of a marriage—of a husband, the consummate Secret Agent, who, she feels, had betrayed "a genuine wife" and "a genuine brother-in-law," as he had betrayed many others, in England and abroad, during the period of eleven years he acted as a secret agent. The death of Stevie marks, for Winnie, the death of an illusion, as she drops "the gold circlet of the wedding ring" into a dustbin.

From this point on the novel moves dramatically to its concluding scenes and chapters (particularly the eleventh chapter, "one of the most astonishing triumphs of genius in fiction," declares Dr. F. R. Leavis).[7] The emphasis in this chapter is on Verloc, not only on some of his inner thoughts regarding the fateful happening, but also on some of the thoughts he expresses to his wife, who is shuddering and hiding her face in her hands. "I didn't mean any harm to come the boy," he insists, for in fact he never expected Stevie to stumble within five minutes of being left to himself. Verloc, too, is a victim of illusion, believing fully in "being loved for himself." Clearly he never understood the depth of his wife's love for her brother, "since it was impossible for him to understand it without ceasing to be himself." Illusions, even the simplest ones, do not easily vanish, as another of Verloc's assertions shows: "Do be reasonable, Winnie. What would it have been if you had lost me?" The unfolding events in *The Secret Agent*, particularly in the concluding chapters, illustrate remarkably the truth of what Joyce Cary, in *Art and Reality*, writes about the moral dimension of art: "A novelist creates a world of action and therefore he has to deal with motive, with morality. . . . The story gives the meaning, the morality."[8]

III

The effects of moral blindness, as the lives and fates of Adolf and Winnie Verloc demonstrate, are staggering. His belief that he has been loyal to his employers, to the cause of social stability, and to his affection embodies grand illusions for which he pays with his life. Clearly, both husband and wife have been dishonest with each other, masking their motives in the most insidious ways: "They refrained from going to the bottom of facts and motives." During their marriage of seven years, he has kept his activities secret from her; and she has never fully admitted to him that she married him only to provide home and security for young and vulnerable Stevie. Winnie thus feels herself to be a betrayed woman; he, the victim of an unexpected catastrophe that ends his career—he is somewhat over the age of forty—as a secret agent, and now suddenly makes him subject to "the knife of infuriated revolutionists." But his career never meant anything to

[7]*The Great Tradition: George Eliot, Henry James, Joseph Conrad* (London, 1960) 214.

[8](New York, 1958) 149, 154.

her, and she knew very little about its complexion and needs. What she did know was that she had to insure Stevie's security at any cost. And the man who now is speaking, her husband, she sees as one who took her brother away from his home *and* from her to murder him. Her "militant love" and care for Stevie are even likened to a big battle, which she has lost because of her husband.

Throughout this agonizing and muted evening encounter, Mrs. Verloc fixes her solitary thoughts on Stevie: "The poor boy had been taken out and killed. The poor boy was dead." And she reaches this unalterable conclusion: "There was no need for her now to stay there, in that kitchen, in that house, with that man—since the boy was gone for ever." The entire encounter is exhausting for Verloc, who flings himself upon the sofa in the parlor, overcome by his wife's "sulking in that dreadful overcharged silence." Winnie, for her part, "remained irresolute, as if scrupulously aware of something wanting . . . for the formal closing of that transaction."

This "closing" comes with catastrophic vengeance in the final pages. No amount of quoting or summarizing can do justice to what unfolds in the story of the Verlocs as all their idols of illusion come crashing down. A tragic poetry triumphs here, of a Shakespearian magnitude. Verloc "reposing [on the sofa] in that pathetic condition of optimism induced by an excess of fatigue," invites Winnie to come and join him, with that peculiar tone that has "the note of wooing." But their love is in essence a corrupt love. Little does he realize her hatred for him, or the power of clarity and cunning and purposefulness that dictates her every thought and gesture of revenge. A macabre suspensefulness permeates this scene, "the formal closing," as Winnie Verloc, who even assumes an uncanny resemblance to Stevie, passes on toward the sofa, where Verloc "was lying on his back and staring upwards." What he sees, almost in chiaroscuro, has frightening impact on him: "He saw partly on the ceiling and partly on the wall the moving shadow of an arm with a clenched hand holding a carving knife." It is now too late for him to dodge the death blow from a woman who "had gone raving mad—murdering mad," as she enacts, with steely alacrity and fierce determination, "Stevie's urgent claim on her devotion." "The knife was already planted in his breast," Conrad writes. "It met no resistance on its way. . . . Mr. Verloc, the Secret Agent, turning slightly on his side with the force of the blow, expired without stirring a limb in the muttered sound of the word 'Don't' by way of protest."

The death of Adolf Verloc marks still another death of illusion. Conrad merges these two states of death with the "Tic, tic, tic" of the clock that

Winnie hears, in the mystery of time, and the dark drops of blood that she sees, in the fact of extinction, falling on the floorcloth. A now frightened but comprehending Winnie ("afraid of the gallows") beholds the sight of her husband: "He was nothing," as we are again reminded by Conrad that illusions and nothingness are synonymous, that illusion ends in nothing. Winnie's own fate, as recorded in these last pages, dramatizes, by reemphasizing, the consequences of illusion. As such her ending emerges as a kind of fictional constatation, that is, as a process of verification. Winnie has thoughts of death, or of escape abroad. The note of nothingness in the novel resounds: "She had nothing. . . . She was alone in London: and the whole town of marvels and mud, with its maze of streets and its mass of lights, was sunk in a hopeless night, rested at the bottom of a black abyss"—the abyss of negations one might add.

Her chance meeting on the street with Comrade Ossipon, "the robust anarchist" inordinately "interested in women," reinforces the constatation. The instinct of self-preservation prompts Winnie to see Ossipon as "a radiant messenger of light." But Ossipon's motives are neither sincere nor benevolent: he is thinking of material benefits, the business value of the shop and the amount of money the widow of Mr. Verloc has in the bank. Ossipon still labors under the misapprehension that it was Verloc who died in Greenwich Park, as he skeptically eyes Mrs. Verloc, "veiled in a black net," hanging on his arm, and entreating him to join her in an immediate flight to the Continent. Increasingly he feels "himself losing his footing in the depths of this tenebrous affair. . . . But there was the rest. These savings. The money!" His hunger for "the money"—"We revolutionists are not rich," he exclaims—prompts him to propose that they take the 10:30 train from the Waterloo Station to Southampton, the boat leaving there for France at about midnight. But Winnie insists that they return first to the shop on Brett Street in order to shut the door, which she had forgotten to do earlier. And so they now return together, he thinking opportunely that she might have left the money in the drawer. The light in the parlor, where Verloc lies dead on the sofa, not having been put out, she asks the revolutionist to tend to this task, even pushing him forward into the parlor.

Discovering Verloc's body, Ossipon rids himself of his misapprehension, and even sees himself as victim of madness. The full sight of Verloc's body makes him retch violently. Now, too, he realizes that Winnie is Verloc's executioner, though he is also "terrified out of all capacity for belief or disbelief in regard to this extraordinary affair." Terror fills him as she begs him to help her, thinking that she possibly has another knife, this time for him. And only now does he realize that it was Stevie, "the degenerate—by heaven!" who got killed. Desperate for a savior, she now entrusts him with the new pigskin pocket-book containing the money Verloc had given to her to tide her over until he finished a probable jail sentence, a consequence he saw as inevitable for his actions as a secret agent. Ossipon, in any case, accompanies her to the Waterloo Station for the train that would then take her to Southampton and the cross-Channel boat for France.

Author of a medical pamphlet, lecturer on social aspects of hygiene to working men's clubs, admirer of Cesare Lombroso's theories on the psychology of the criminal, especially the relation between a criminal's physical constitution and his pathological nature, Ossipon views Winnie "scientifically" as an atavistic criminal: "the sister of a degenerate, a degenerate herself—of a murdering type." Eventually they enter one of the empty compartments of the train, which soon begins to move. "He felt the train roll quickly, rumbling heavily to the sound of the woman's loud sobs, and then crossing the carriage in two long strides he opened the door deliberately, and leaped out." Comrade Ossipon, anarchist, "flush of safe banknotes as never before in his life," makes his escape—a savior neither to Winnie Verloc nor to mankind. His actions further exemplify the truth of the words of one critic, Chull Wang: "What the anarchists are doing in the society is an outrageous betrayal of humanity."[9] Of the fate of Winnie Verloc, we finally learn from these last lines of a paragraph in a newspaper account, ten days old, under the caption, "Suicide of Lady Passenger from a cross-Channel Boat": "An impenetrable mystery seems destined to hang for ever over this act of madness or despair."

IV

The concluding chapter of *The Secret Agent* finds Ossipon and the professor, "the Perfect Anarchist," together in the latter's shoddy room. Their discussion in the room and then during their omnibus ride to and the time they spend in the Silenus Restaurant underlines the moral debasement

---

[9]See chap. 4, "*The Secret Agent,*" in Chull Wang, "Betrayal and Moral Imagination: A Study of Joseph Conrad's Five Major Works" (diss., College Park MD, 1990). I am indebted to Dr. Wang for his many and rich insights into Conrad's views and treatment of moral issues in the major novels (*Lord Jim*, *Nostromo*, *The Secret Agent*, *Under Western Eyes*, and *Victory*).

that the anarchists and their actions personify. The professor wants to exterminate first "the great multitude of the weak" as the source of the world's problems, with only the professor remaining as a saving force. Ossipon, on the other hand, speaks of eternity as "a damned hole." The entire conversation is no less morose than their immediate surroundings. Ossipon is in a state of total confusion and knows not where he is going, not even thinking of adding to his "collection of women." The note of nothingness rings out again in the penultimate paragraph of the novel: "Comrade Ossipon walked without looking where he put his feet, feeling no fatigue, feeling nothing, seeing nothing. . . . " The "incorruptible Professor" is also seen, in the very last paragraph, "averting his eyes from the odious multitude of mankind. He had no future." His thoughts, Conrad tells us, "caressed the images of ruin and destruction," as he walked "terrible in the simplicity of his idea calling madness and despair to the regeneration of the world."

From a dramatic point of view *The Secret Agent* could have ended, powerfully, with the murder of Verloc. But such an ending would be too simplistic in its melodrama. A moral tale requires dramatic commentation that more directly involves the reader in deliberation and judgment, appropriate to the purpose and scope of a moral tale. In the last two chapters of *The Secret Agent*, which form a kind of coda, Conrad is making sure that his reader will not be lulled by the visual power and verbal magic of the novel. There are serious lessons that have to be registered, and moral judgments that have to be crystallized with absolute decisiveness of meaning. Conrad's allegiance to the moral imagination receives added confirmation here. Clearly he is aware that a reader should not "walk in darkness," and that it is the novelist's task to help the reader pass beyond "the shadow-line" in facing up to ultimate moral issues.

In the working of the revolutionary mind Conrad recreates the abstract and perverse forms of ideology, which Russell Kirk defines as "a passionate endeavor to overthrow the spiritual and moral order."[10] Conrad enables a modern reader to see anarchism as the consummation of nihilism and its program of absolute denial and rejection of life and spirit. The ideology of anarchism, as this novel's events and outcome bear out, completes and advances nihilism to its ultimate point of negation through destruction.

---

[10] *Enemies of the Permanent Things: Observations of Abnormity in Literature and Politics* (La Salle IL, 1969) 164.

Anarchy is what comes beyond nihilism: the final outrage, the final debasement, the final apostasy. Anarchy can thus be called the final movement of revolution and terror, as one astute interpreter observes, in short, the end-stage when anarchism brings the movement which nihilism began to its logical conclusion.[11] Indeed, the anarchists in *The Secret Agent* represent a subhumanism in which madness and despair prevail and rule.

In *The Secret Agent* Conrad is neither preacher nor propagandist; he is a master of art-speech, intuitively and tensively responsive to social and moral issues, which he renders in plot, action, scene, dialogue, character. "The function of the novelist," again to recall Joyce Cary, "is to make the world contemplate and understand itself, not only as rational being but as experience of value, as a complete thing."[12] Joseph Conrad fulfills this function, this responsibility, in *The Secret Agent*. If Conrad is concerned with the order of human destiny, he is also concerned with the order of the human soul. *The Secret Agent* gives us an astonishing picture of what has gone wrong with the order of the soul in the "antagonist world" in which "the imperative of relevance" discards life of the soul. The "sordid surroundings and the moral squalor of the tale," to use Conrad's words, "lie simply in the outward circumstances of the setting." It is as a moral tale that *The Secret Agent* enters and illuminates the inward terrain.

In the writing of this novel, Conrad insisted, "I was simply attending to my business. . . . with complete self-surrender"—in other words, with complete concentration, purposefulness, seriousness, honesty. These qualities, which are the stuff of the moral imagination, command a great novelist to speak to our time, to our condition, to our conscience—and to our soul.

---

[11]Eugene (Fr. Seraphim) Rose, *Nihilism: The Root of the Revolution of the Modern Age* (Forestville CA, 1994) 88. For a discussion of this book, see my review, "On Spiritual Disorder," *Modern Age: A Quarterly Review* (Winter 1996): 207-10.

[12]Joyce Cary, "Morality and the Novelist," in *Selected Essays*, ed. A. G. Bishop (New York, 1976) 153.

Chapter 2

Lord Jim

Lord Jim (1900), Joseph Conrad's fourth novel, is the story of a ship which collides with "a floating derelict" and will doubtlessly "go down at any moment" during a "silent black squall." The ship, old and rust-eaten, known as the *Patna*, is voyaging across the Indian Ocean to the Red Sea. Aboard are eight hundred Muslim pilgrims who are being transported to a "holy place, the promise of salvation, the reward of eternal life." Terror possesses the captain and several of his officers, who jump from the pilgrim-ship and thus wantonly abandon the sleeping passengers who are unaware of their peril. For crew members in the safety of their lifeboat, dishonor is better than death.

Beyond the immediate details and the effects of a shipwreck, this novel portrays, in the words of the story's narrator, Captain Marlow, "those struggles of an individual trying to save from the fire his idea of what his moral identity should be. . . . " That individual is a young seaman, Jim, who serves as the chief mate of the *Patna* and who also "jumps." Recurringly Jim envisions himself as "always an example of devotion to duty and as unflinching as a hero in a book." But his heroic dream of "saving people from sinking ships, cutting away masts in a hurricane, swimming through a surf with a line," does not square with what he really represents: one who falls from grace, and whose "crime" is "a breach of faith with the community of mankind." Jim's aspirations and actions underline the disparity between idea and reality, or what is generally termed "indissoluble contradictions of being." His is also the story of a man in search of some form of atonement once he recognizes that his "avidity for adventure, and in a sense of many-sided courage," and his dream of "the success of his imaginary achievements," constitute a romantic illusion.

Jim's leap from the *Patna* generates in him a severe moral crisis that forces him to "come round to the view that only a meticulous precision of statement would bring out the true horror behind the appalling face of things." It is especially hard for Jim to confront this "horror" since his confidence in "his own superiority" seems so absolute. The "*Patna* affair" compels him in the end to peer into his deepest self and then to relinquish "the charm and innocence of illusions." The Jim of the *Patna* undergoes "the ordeal of the fiery furnace," as he is severely tested "by those events of the sea that show in the light of the day the inner worth of a man, the edge of his temper, and the fibre of his stuff; that reveal the quality of his resistance and the secret truth of his pretences, not only to others but also to himself." Clearly the *Patna* is, for Jim, the experience both of a moment and of a lifetime.

This novel, from beginning to end, is the story of Jim; throughout the focus is on his life and character, on what he has done, or not done, on his crime and punishment, his failure of nerve as a seaman. It is, as well, the story of his predicament and his fate, the destiny of his soul—of high expectations and the great "chance missed," of "wasted opportunity" and "what he had failed to obtain," all the result of leaving his post, and abdicating his responsibility. Thus we see him in an unending moment of crisis, "overburdened by the knowledge of an imminent death" as he imagines the grim scene before him: "He stood still looking at those recumbent bodies, a doomed man aware of his fate, surveying the silent company of the dead! Nothing could save them!"

For Jim the overwhelming question, "What could I do—what?," brings the answer of "Nothing!" The *Patna*, as it plows the Arabian Sea ("smooth and cool to the eye like a sheet of ice") on its way to the Red Sea, is close to sinking, with its engines stopped, the steam blowing off, its deep rumble making "the whole night vibrate like a bass string." Jim's imagination conjures up a dismal picture of a catastrophe that is inescapable and merciless. It is not that Jim thinks so much of saving himself as it is the tyranny of his belief that there are eight hundred people on ship—and only seven lifeboats. Conrad's storyteller, Marlow, much sympathetic to Jim's plight, discerns in him an affliction of helplessness that compounds his sense of hopelessness, making Jim incapable of confronting total shipwreck, as he envisions "a ship floating head down, checked in sinking by a sheet of old iron too rotten to stand being shored up." But Jim is a victim not only of his imagination, but also of what Conrad calls a "moral situation of enslavement." So torn and defeated is Jim, that his soul itself also seems possessed by some "invisible personality, an antagonistic and inseparable partner of his existence."

Jim's acceptance of the inevitability of disaster and his belief that he could do absolutely nothing to forestall the loss of eight hundred passengers render him helpless, robbing him of any ability to take any kind of lifesaving action—"I thought I might just as well stand where I was and wait." In short, in Jim we discern a disarmed man who surrenders his will to action. The gravity of Jim's situation is so overwhelming that it leaves him, his heroic aspirations notwithstanding, in a state of paralysis. His predicament, then, becomes his moral isolation and desolation, one in which Jim's "desire of peace waxes stronger as hope declines . . . and conquers the very desire of life." He gives in at precisely the point when strenuous effort and decisive actions are mandated, so as to resist "unreasonable forces." His frame of mind recalls here Jean-Paul Sartre's pertinent comment, in *The Age of Reason* (1945), "That's what existence means: draining one's own self dry without a sense of thrust."

Everything in Jim's background points to his success as a career seaman. We learn that, one of five sons, he originally came from a parsonage, from one of those "abodes of piety and peace," in England; his vocation for the sea emerged early on and, for a period of two years, he served on a "training ship for affairs of the mercantile marine." His station was in the foretop of a training ship chained to her moorings. We learn that, on one occasion, in the dusk of a winter's day, a gale suddenly blew forth with a savage fury of wind and rain and tide, endangering the small craft on the shore and the ferryboats anchored in the harbor, as well as the training ship itself. The force of the gale "made him hold his breath in awe. He stood still. It seemed to him he was whirled around. He was jostled." We learn, too, that a coaster, in search of shelter, crashed through a schooner at anchor. We see the cutter now tossing abreast the ship, hovering dangerously. Jim is on the point of leaping overboard to save a man overboard, but fails to do so. There is "pain of conscious defeat in his eyes," as the captain shouts to Jim. "Too late, youngster. . . . Better luck next time. This will teach you to be smart."

This incident, related in the first chapter of the novel, serves to prepare us for Jim's actions later on the *Patna*, and also suggests a kind of flaw in Jim's behavior in a moment of danger. Early on in his career, then, Jim had displayed a willingness to "flinch" from his obligations, thus revealing a defect in the heroism about which he romanticized and which led him to creating self-serving fantasies and illusions. "He felt angry with the brutal tumult of earth and sky for taking him unawares and checking unfairly a generous readiness for narrow escapes." Jim, as a seaman, refuses to admit his fear of fear, and in this he shows an inclination to escape the truth of reality by "putting out of sight all the reminders of our folly, of our weakness, of our mortality." Clearly the episode on the training ship serves both as a symptom and as a portent, underscores an inherent element of failure and disgrace in Jim's character that, in the course of the novel, he must confront if he is to transcend the dreams and illusions that beguile him, and that he must finally vanquish if he is to find his "moral identity." His early experience on the training ship makes him a marked man. It remains for his experience later on the *Patna* to make him a "condemned man."

That nothing rests secure, that, in the midst of certitude, danger lurks, that peace and contentment are at the mercy of the whirl of the world, are inescapable conditions of human existence. These daunting dichotomies, as we find them depicted in *Lord Jim*, are forever teasing and testing humans in their life journey. Conrad sees these dichotomies in the unfolding spectacle of man and nature. To evince the enormous power of this process Conrad chooses to render time in a continuum which fills all space. Time has no end, no *telos*; it absorbs beginnings and endings—the past, present, and future not only in their connections but also in their disconnections.

Conrad's spatial technique is no less complex, and no less revealing, than his use of time. Hence, he employs spatial dimension so as to highlight Jim's sense of guilt in jumping from the *Patna*. A "seaman in exile from the sea," Jim is constantly in flight when his incognito is repeatedly broken by the knowledge of his *Patna* connection. For years this "fact followed him casually but inevitably," whenever and wherever he retreated. Jim's "keen perception of the Intolerable" finally drives him away for good from seaports and white men, "into the virgin forest, the Malays of the jungle village." The "acute consciousness of lost honor," as Conrad expresses it in his "Author's Note," is Jim's burden of fate. And wherever he retreats he is open to attack from some "deadly snake in every brush." Time as memory and place as torment become his twin oppressors.

The specificities of the *Patna* episode were to come out during a well-attended Official Court of Inquiry that takes place for several days in early August 1883. Most of the details, in the form of remarks and commentaries, are supplied by Marlow in his long oral narrative, especially as these emerge from Jim's own confession to Marlow when they happen to meet after the proceedings, on the yellow portico of the Malabar House. Humiliated and broken, his certificate revoked, his career destroyed, Jim can never return to his home and face his father—"I could never explain. He wouldn't understand." Again and again, in his confession, Jim shows feelings of desperation and even hysteria: "Everything had betrayed him!" For him it is imperative to be identified neither with the "odious and fleshly" German skipper, Gustav, "the incarnation of everything vile and base that lurks in the world we love," nor with the chief and the second engineers, "skunks" who are extensions of the captain's coarseness and cowardice.

But that, in fact, Jim does jump overboard—"a jump into the unknown"—and in effect joins them in deserting the *Patna* ultimately agonizes his moral sense and impels him to scrutinize that part of his being in which the element of betrayal has entered. By such an action he feels contaminated, unclean, disgraced. How to separate himself morally from the captain and his engineers is still another cruel question to which he must find an answer. In this respect, Jim reminds us of the tragic heroes in ancient Greek drama whose encounters with destiny entail both risks and moral instruction. "We begin to live," Conrad reminds us, "when we have conceived life as a tragedy."

How does one "face the darkness"? How does one behave to the unknowable? These are other basic questions that vex Jim. He wants, of course, to answer these affirmatively, or at least to wrestle with them in redeeming ways, even as he appears to see himself within a contradiction—as one who can have no place in the universe once he has failed to meet the standards of his moral code. Refusing to accept any "helping hand" extended to him to "clear out," he decides to "fight this thing down," to expiate his sin, in short, to suffer penitently the agony of his failure: "He had loved too well to imagine himself a glorious racehorse, and now he was condemned to toil without honour like a costermonger's donkey." Jim's innermost sufferings revolve precisely around his perception of his loss of honor, of his surrender to cowardice. The crushing shame of this perception tortures Jim, without respite. " 'I had jumped—hadn't I?' he asked [Marlow], dismayed. 'That's what I had to live down.' "

Jim's moral sense is clearly outraged by his actions. This outrage wracks his high conception of himself, compelling him in time to see himself outside of his reveries that Conrad also associates with "the determination to lounge safely through existence." What clouds Jim's fate is that such a net of safety and certitude has no sustained reality. Within the serenity that seemed to bolster his thoughts of "valorous deeds" there are hidden menaces that assault his self-contentment and self-deception and abruptly awaken Jim to his actual condition and circumstances. In one way, it can be said, Jim is a slave of the "idyllic imagination" (as Irving Babbitt calls it), with its expansive appetites, chimeras, reveries, pursuit of illusion. Jim's is the story of a man who comes to discern not only the pitfalls of this imagination but also the need to free himself from its bondage. But to free himself from bondage requires of Jim painstaking effort, endurance. He must work diligently to transform chimeric, if incipient, fortitude into an active virtue as it interacts with a world that, like the *Patna*, can be "full of reptiles"—a world in which "not one of us is safe."

Conrad uses Jim to delineate the moral process of recovery. As such, Conrad delineates the paradigms of this process as these evolve in the midst of much anguish and laceration, leading to the severest scrutiny and judgment of the total human personality. Jim pays attention, in short, to the immobility of his soul; it will take much effort for him to determine where he is and what is happening to him if he is to emerge from the "heart of darkness" and the affliction within and around him to face what is called "the limiting moment." It is, in an inherently spiritual context, a moment of repulsion when one examines the sin in oneself, and hates it. His sense of repulsion is tantamount to moral renunciation, as he embarks on the path to recovery from the romantic habit of daydreaming.

In the end Jim comes to despise his condition, acceding as he does to the moral imperative. He accepts the need to see his "trouble" as his own, and he instinctively volunteers to answer questions regarding the *Patna* by appearing before the Official Court of Inquiry "held in the police court of an Eastern port." (This actually marks his first encounter with Marlow, who is in attendance and who seems to be sympathetically aware of "his hopeless difficulty.") He gives his testimony fully, objectively, honestly, as he faces the presiding magistrate. The physical details of Jim's appearance underscore his urge "to go on talking for truth's sake, perhaps for his own sake"—"fair of face, big of frame, with young, gloomy eyes, he held his shoulders upright above the box while his soul writhed within him." Marlow's reaction to Jim is instinctively positive: "I liked his appearance; he came from the right place; he was one of us." In striking ways, Jim is a direct contrast to the other members of "the *Patna* gang": "They were nobodies," in Marlow's words.

It should be recalled here that Jim adamantly refused to help the others put the lifeboat clear of the ship and get it into the water for their escape. Indeed, as Jim insists to Marlow, he wanted to keep his distance from the deserters, for there was "nothing in common between him and these men." Their frenzied, self-serving actions to abandon the ship and its human cargo infuriated Jim—"I loathed them. I hated them." The scene depicting the abandonment of the *Patna* is one filled with "the turmoil of terror," dramatizing the contrast between Jim and the other officers—between honor and dishonor, loyalty and disloyalty, in short, between aspiration and descent on the larger metaphysical map of human behavior. Jim personifies resistance to the negative as he tries to convey to Marlow "the brooding rancour of his mind into the bare recital of events." Jim's excruciating moral effort not to join the others and to ignore their desperate motions is also pictured at a critical moment when he felt the *Patna* dangerously dipping her bows, and then lifting them gently, slowly—"and ever so little."

The reality of a dangerous situation now seems to be devouring Jim, as he was once again to capitulate to the inner voice of weakness and doubt telling him to "leap" from the *Patna*. Futility hovers ominously around Jim at this last moment when death arrives in the form of a third engineer "clutch[ing] at the air with raised arms, totter[ing] and collaps[ing]." A terrified, transfixed Jim finds himself stumbling over the legs of the dead man lying on the bridge. And from the lifeboat below three voices yelled out eerily—"one bleated, another screamed, one howled"—imploring the man to jump, not realizing of course that he was dead of a heart attack: "Jump, George! Jump! Oh, jump. . . . We'll catch you! Jump! . . . Geo-o-o-orge! Oh, jump!" This desperate, screeching verbal command clearly pierces Jim's internal condition of fear and terror, just as the ship again seemed to begin a slow plunge, with rain sweeping over her "like a broken sea." And once again Jim is unable to sustain his refusal to betray his idea of honor. Here his body and soul are caught in the throes of still another "chance missed."

The assaults of nature on Jim's outer situation are as vicious at this pivotal point of his life as are the assaults of conscience on his moral sense. These clashing outer and inner elements are clearly pushing Jim to the edge, as heroic aspiration and human frailty wrestle furiously for the possession of his soul. What happens will have permanent consequences for him, as Conrad reveals here, with astonishing power of perception. Here, then, we discern a process of cohesion and dissolution, when Jim's fate seems to be vibrating unspeakably as he experiences the radical pressures and tensions of his struggle to be more than what he is, or what he aspires to be. Jim, as if replacing the dead officer lying on the deck of the *Patna*, jumps: "It had happened somehow . . . , " Conrad writes. "He had landed partly on somebody and fallen across a thwart." He was now in the boat with those he loathed; "[h]e had tumbled from a height he could never scale again." "I wished I could die," he admits to Marlow. "There was no going back. It was as if I had jumped into a well—into an everlasting deep hole."

A cold, thick rain and "a pitchy blackness" weigh down the lurching boat; "it was like being swept by a flood through a cavern." Crouched down in the bows, Jim fearfully discerns the *Patna*, "just one yellow gleam of the masthead light high up and blurred like a last star ready to dissolve." And then all is black, as one of the deserters cries out shakily, "She's gone!" Those in the boat remain quiet, and a strange silence prevails all around them, blurring the sea and the sky, with "nothing to see and nothing to hear." To Jim it seemed as if everything was gone, all was over. The other three shipmates in the boat mistake him for George, and when they do recognize him they are startled and curse him. The boat itself seems filled with hatred, suspicion, villainy, betrayal. "We were like men walled up quick in a roomy grave," Jim confides to Marlow.

The boat itself epitomizes abject failure and alienation from mankind. Everything in it and around it mirrors Jim's schism of soul, "imprisoned in the solitude of the sea." Through the varying repetition of language and images Conrad accentuates Jim's distraught inner condition, especially the shame that rages in him for being "in the same boat" with men who exemplify a fellowship of liars. By the time they are picked up just before sunset by the *Avondale*, the captain and his two officers had already "made up a story" that would sanction their desertion of the *Patna*, which in fact had not sunk and which, with its pilgrims, had been safely towed to Aden by a French gunboat, eventually to end her days in a breaking-up yard. Unlike the others, Jim would choose to face the full consequences of his actions, "to face it out—alone for myself—wait for another chance—find out. . . . "

"Jim's affair" was destined to live on years later in the memories and minds of men, as instanced by Marlow's chance meeting in a Sydney café with a now elderly French lieutenant who was a boarding-officer from the gunboat and remained on the *Patna* for thirty hours. For Marlow this meeting was "a moment of vision" that enables him to penetrate more deeply into the events surrounding the *Patna* as he discusses them with one who had been "there." The French officer, at this time the third lieutenant on the flagship of the French Pacific squadron, and Marlow, now commanding a merchant vessel, thus share their recollections, from which certain key thoughts emerge, measuring and clarifying the entire affair. The two men here bring to mind a Greek chorus speaking words of wisdom that explain human suffering and tragedy. In essence it is Jim's predicament that Conrad wants to diagnose here so as to enlist the reader's understanding, even sympathy. "The fear, the fear—look you—it is always there," the French officer declares. And he goes on to say to Marlow—all of this with reference to Jim: "And what life may be worth . . . when the honor is gone. . . . I can offer no opinion—because—monsieur—I know nothing of it."

For Conrad the task of the novelist is to illuminate "Jim's case" for the reader's judgment, and he does this, from diverse angles and levels, in order for the reader to consider all of the evidence, all the ambivalences, antinomies, paradoxes. If for Jim the struggle is to ferret out his true moral identity, for the reader the task is to meditate on what is presented to him and, in the end, to attain a transcendent apprehension of life in time and life by values.[1] Jim is, to repeat, "one of us," and in him we meet and see ourselves on moral grounds, so to speak.

In the final paragraph of his "Author's Note," Conrad is careful to point out that the creation of Jim "is not the product of coldly perverted thinking." Nor is he "a figure of Northern mists." In Jim, Conrad sees Everyman. In short, he is the creative outgrowth of what Irving Babbitt terms "the high seriousness of the ethical imagination," and not of the "idyllic imagination," with its distortions of human character. In other words, this is the "moral imagination" which imitates the universal and reveres the "Permanent Things." In Jim we participate in and perceive a normative consciousness, as we become increasingly aware of Jim's purposive function in reflective prose and poetic fiction, aspiring as it does to make transcendence perceptible.[2] Conrad testifies to the force and truth of the principles of a metaphysics of art when, in the concluding sentence of his "Author's Note," he writes about his own chance encounter with the Jim in ourselves: "One morning in the commonplace surroundings of an Eastern roadstead, I saw his form pass by—appealing—significant—under a cloud—perfectly silent. Which is as it should be. It was for me, with all the sympathy of which I was capable, to seek fit words for his meaning. He was 'one of us.' " A man of "indomitable resolution," Jim strikes aside any "plan for evasion" proffered to him by a "helping hand" like Marlow's. Nothing can tempt him to ignore the consequences of both his decisions and indecisions, which surround him like "deceitful ghosts, austere shades." Any plan to save him from "degradation, ruin, and despair" he shuns, choosing instead to endure the conditions of homelessness and aloneness. He refuses to identify with any schemes or schemers of a

---

[1]See the chapter "Toward a Metaphysics of Art," in my book *The Reverent Discipline: Essays in Literary Criticism and Culture* (Knoxville TN, 1974) 185-204.

[2]See Russell Kirk, "The Perversity of Recent Fiction: Reflections on the Moral Imagination," *Redeeming the Time* (Wilmington DE, 1996) 68-86.

morally insensitive nature. The "deep idea" in him is the moral sense to which he somehow hangs on and to the innermost voice of which he listens.

Unfailingly Conrad reveals to us the nature of Jim's character and will in a "narrative [which] moves through a devious course of identifications and distinctions," as one critic observes.[3] Thus in the person of Captain Montague Brierly we have a paragon sailing-ship skipper, and an august member of the board of inquiry, whose overarching self-satisfaction and self-worth presented to Marlow and to the world itself "a surface as hard as granite." Unexplainably, however, Brierly commits suicide a week after the official inquiry ended by jumping overboard, less than three days after his vessel left port on his outward passage. It seems, as Marlow believes, that with "something akin to fear of the immensity of his contempt for the young man [Jim] under examination, he was probably holding silent inquiry into his own case." Jim will not go the way of Brierly, whose juxtaposition to Jim, early on in the novel, serves to emphasize the young seaman's fund of inner strength needed to resist perversion of the moral sense. Unlike Brierly, Jim will not be unjust to himself by trivializing his soul.

Nor will Jim become part of any business scheme that would conveniently divert him from affirming the moral sense. A farfetched and obviously disastrous business venture ("[a]s good as a gold-mine"), concocted by Marlow's slight acquaintance, a West Australian by the name of Chester, and his partner, "Holy-Terror Robinson," further illustrates in Jim the ascendancy of "his fine sensibilities, his fine feelings, his fine longings." Jim will not be identified with the unsavory Chester any more than he would be identified with the *Patna* gang. Marlow himself, whatever mixed feelings he may have as to Jim's weaknesses, intuits that Jim has nobler aspirations than being "thrown to the dogs" and in effect to "slip away into the darkness" with Chester. Jim's destiny may be tragic, but it is not demeaning or tawdry, which in the end sums up Marlow's beneficent trust in Jim.

In a state of disgrace, Jim was to work as a ship-chandler for various firms, but he was always on the run—to Bombay, to Calcutta, to Rangoon, to Penang, to Bangkok, to Batavia, moving from firm to firm, always "under the shadow" of his connection to the *Patna* "skunks." Always, too, the paternal Marlow was striving to find "opportunities" for Jim. Persisting in these efforts, Marlow pays a visit to an acquaintance of his, Stein, an

---

[3]See Dorothy Van Ghent, *The English Novel: Form and Function* (New York, 1953) 229-44.

aging, successful merchant-adventurer who owns a large interisland business in the Malay Archipelago with a lot of trading posts in out-of-the-way trading places for collecting produce. Bavarian-born Stein is, for Marlow, "one of the most trustworthy men" who can help to mitigate Jim's plight. A famous entomologist and a "learned collector" of beetles and butterflies, he lives in Samarang. A sage, as well, he ponders on the problems of human existence: "Man is amazing, but he is not a masterpiece . . . man is come where he is not wanted, where there is no place for him. . . . " he says to Marlow. He goes on to observe that man "wants to be a saint, and he wants to be a devil," and even sees himself, "in a dream," "as a very fine fellow—so fine as he can never be. . . . " Solemnly, he makes this observation, so often quoted from Conrad's writings: "A man that is born falls into a dream like a man who falls into the sea. . . . The way is to the destructive element submit yourself, and with the exertions of your hands and feet in the water make the deep, deep sea keep you up."

Marlow's meeting with Stein provides for a philosophical probing of some of the fundamental ideas and life-issues Conrad presents in *Lord Jim*. The human condition, no less than the kingdom of nature, is the province of his explorations. His musings on the mysteries of existence ultimately have the aim of enlarging our understanding of Jim's character and soul. These musings also have the effect of heightening Jim's struggles to find his true moral identity. Inevitably, abstraction and ambiguity are inherent elements in Stein's metaphysics, so to speak, even as his persona and physical surroundings merge to project a kind of mystery; his spacious apartment, Marlow recalls, "melted into shapeless gloom like a cavern." Indeed Marlow's visit to Stein is like a visit to a medical diagnostician who possesses holistic powers of discernment—"our conference resembled so much a medical consultation—Stein of learned aspect sitting in an armchair before his desk. . . . " Stein's ruminations, hence, have at times an oracular dimension, as "his voice . . . seemed to roll voluminous and grave—mellowed by distance." It is in this solemn atmosphere, and with subdued tones, that Stein delivers his chief pronouncement on Jim: " 'He is romantic—romantic,' he repeated. 'And that is very bad—very bad. . . . Very good, too,' he added."

The encounter with Stein assumes, almost at the mid-point of the novel, episodic significance in Jim's moral destiny, and in the final journey of a soul in torment. Stein's observations, insightful as they are, hardly penetrate the depths of Jim's soul, its conditions and circumstances, which defy rational analysis and formulaic prescriptions. The soul has its own life, along with but also beyond the outer life Stein images. It must answer to new demands, undertake new functions, face new situations—and experience new trials. The dark night of the soul is at hand, inexorably, as Jim retreats to Patusan, one of the Malay islands, known to officials in Batavia for "its irregularities and aberrations." It is as if Jim had now been sent "into a star of the fifth magnitude." Behind him he leaves his "earthly failings." "Let him creep twenty feet underground and stay there," to recall Brierly's words. In Patusan, at a point of the river forty miles from the sea, Jim will relieve a Portuguese by the name of Cornelius, Stein & Co.'s manager there. It is as if Stein and Marlow had schemed to "tumble" him into another world, "to get him out of the way; out of his own way." "Disposed" of, Jim thus enters spiritual exile, alone and friendless, a straggler, a hermit in the wilderness of Patusan, where "all sound and all movements in the world seemed to come to an end."

The year in which Jim, now close to thirty years of age, arrives in Patusan is 1886, where the political situation is unstable—"utter insecurity for life and property was the normal condition." Dirt, stench, and mud-stained natives are the conditions with which Jim must deal. In the midst of all of this rot, Jim, in white apparel, "appeared like a creature not only of another kind but of another essence." In Patusan, he soon becomes known as Lord Jim (Tuan Jim), and his work gives him "the certitude of rehabilitation." Patusan, as such, heralds Jim's unceasing attempt to start with a clean slate. But in Patusan, as on the *Patna*, Jim is in extreme peril, for he has to grapple with fiercely opposing native factions: the forces of Doramin, Stein's old friend, chief of the second power in Patusan, and those of Rajah Allang, a brutish chief, constantly locked in quarrels over trade, leading to bloody outbreaks and casualities. Jim's chief goal was "to conciliate imbecile jealousies, and argue away all sorts of senseless mistrusts." Doramin and his "distinguished son," Dain Waris, believe in Jim's "audacious plan." But will he succeed, or will he repeat past failures? Is Chester, to recall his earlier verdict on Jim, going to be right: "He is no earthly good for anything." And will Jim, once and for all, exorcise the "unclean spirits" in himself, with the decisiveness needed for atonement? These are convergent questions that badger Jim in the last three years of his life.

During the Patusan sequence, Jim attains much power and influence: "He dominated the forest, the secular gloom, the old mankind." As a result of Jim's leadership, old Doramin's followers rout their sundry enemies, led not only by the Rajah but also by the vagabond Sherif Ali, an Arab half-breed whose wild men terrorized the land. Jim becomes a legend that gives him even supernatural powers. Lord Jim's word was now "the one truth of every passing day." Certainly, from the standpoint of heroic feats and sheer physical courage and example, Jim was to travel a long way from *Patna* to Patusan. Here his fame is "Immense! . . . the seal of success upon his words, the conquered ground for the soles of his feet, the blind trust of men, the belief in himself snatched from the fire, the solitude of his achievement." If his part in the *Patna* affair led to the derision that pursued him in his flights to nowhere, fame and adoration now define his newly-won greatness. The tarnished first mate of the *Patna* in the Indian Ocean is now the illustrious Lord Jim of the forests of Patusan.

The difficult situations that Jim must now confront in Patusan demand responsible actions, which Conrad portrays with all their complexities and tensions. There is no pause in Jim's constant wrestle with responsibilities, whether to the pilgrims on the *Patna* or the natives in Patusan. The moral pressures on him never ease, requiring of Jim concrete gestures that measure his moral worth. Incessantly he takes moral soundings of himself and of the outer life. The stillness and silences of the physical world have a way of accentuating Jim's inner anguish. He is profoundly aware that some "floating derelict" is waiting stealthily to strike at the roots of order, whether of man or of society.

In the course of relating the events in Patusan, where he was visiting Jim, Marlow speaks of Jim's love for a Eurasian girl, Jewel, who becomes his mistress. Cornelius, the "awful Malacca Portuguese," is Jewel's legal guardian, having married her late mother after her separation from the father of the girl. A "mean, cowardly scoundrel," Cornelius is another repulsive beetle in Jim's life. The enemies from without, like the enemy from within, seem to pursue Jim relentlessly. In Patusan, thus, Cornelius, resentful of being replaced as Stein's representative in the trading post, hates Jim, never stops slandering him, wants him out of the way: "He knows nothing, honorable sir—nothing whatever. Who is he? What does he want here—the big thief? . . . He is a big fool. . . . He's no more than a little child here—like a little child—a little child." Cornelius asks Marlow to intercede with Jim in his favor, so that he might be awarded some "moderate provision—suitable present," since "he regarded himself as entitled to some money, in exchange for the girl." But Marlow is not fazed by Cornelius's imprecations: "He couldn't possibly matter . . . since I had made up my mind that Jim, for whom alone I cared, had at last mastered his fate. . . . " Nor is Jim himself troubled by Cornelius's unseemly presence and the possible danger he presents: "It did not matter who suspected him, who trusted him, who loved him, who hated him. . . . 'I came here to set my back against the wall, and I am going to stay here,' " Jim insists to Marlow.

The concluding movement of the novel, a kind of andante, conveys a "sense of ending." Marlow's long narrative, in fact, is now coming to an end, confluent with his "last talk" with Jim and his own imminent departure from Patusan. The language belongs to the end-time, and is pervaded by deepening sorrow and pity, and by an implicit recognition "of the implacable destiny of which we are the victims—and the tools." A poetry of lamentation takes hold of these pages, and the language is brooding, ominous, recondite. Concurrently, the figure of Cornelius weaves in and out and gives "an inexpressible effect of stealthiness, of dark and secret slinking. . . . His slow, laborious walk resembled the creeping of a repulsive beetle. . . . " We realize that Marlow and Jim will never meet again, as we witness a twilight scene of departure. Having accompanied Marlow as far as the mouth of the river, Jim now watches the schooner taking Marlow to the other world "fall off and gather headway." Marlow sees Jim's figure slowly disappearing, "no bigger than a child—then only a speck, a tiny white speck . . . in a darkened world."

At the end of the novel, Jim finds himself a prisoner and ultimately a victim of treachery as he fights against invading outcasts and desperadoes who, for any price, kill living life—cutthroats led by "the Scourge of God," "Gentleman Brown," a supreme incarnation of evil that Jim must confront. Conrad renders the power of evil in unalleviating ways, even as he sees man's moral poverty as an inescapable reality. Indeed, what makes Jim's fate so overpowering is that he never stops struggling against the ruthless forces of destruction that embody Conrad's vision of evil. What Jim has accomplished in Patusan by creating a more stable social community will now be subject to attack by invaders of "undisguised ruthlessness" who would leave Patusan "strewn over with corpses and enveloped in flames." If Jim's inner world, in the first part of the novel, is in turmoil, it is the outer world, in the second part of the novel, that is collapsing "into a ruin reeking with blood." What we hear in the concluding five chapters of *Lord Jim* is the braying voice of universal discord, crying out with a merciless conviction that, between the men of the Bugis nation living in Patusan and the white marauders, "there would be no faith, no compassion, no speech, no peace."

The last word of the story of Jim's life is reserved for one of Marlow's earlier listeners, "the privileged man," who receives a thick packet of handwritten materials, of which an explanatory letter by Marlow is the most illuminating. A narrative in epistolary form provides us, two years following the completion of Marlow's oral narrative, with the details of the last episode that had "come" to Jim. What Marlow has done is to fit together the fragmentary pieces of Jim's "astounding adventure" so as to record "an intelligible picture" of the last year of his life. The epistolary narrative here is based on the exploits of "a man called Brown," upon whom Marlow happened to come in a wretched Bangkok hovel a few hours before Brown died. The latter was thus to volunteer information that helped complete the story of Jim's life, in which Brown himself played a final and fatal role.

The son of a baronet, Brown is famous for leading a "lawless life," "a latter-day buccaneer," known for his "vehement scorn for mankind at large and for victims in particular." We learn that he hung around the Philippines in his rotten schooner, which, eventually, "he sails into Jim's history, a blind accomplice of the Dark Powers." Their meeting takes place as they face each other across a muddy creek—"standing on the opposite poles of that conception of life which includes all mankind." This encounter is of enormous consequence, as Jim, "the white lord," contends verbally with the "terrible," "sneering" Brown, who slyly invokes their "common blood, an assumption of common experience, a sickening suggestion of common guilt. . . . " The conversation, Marlow was to recall in his letter, appeared "as the deadliest kind of duel on which Fate looked on with her cold-eyed knowledge of the end." Brown, with his "satanic gift of finding out the best and the weakest spot in his victims," seems to be surveying and staking out Jim's character and capability. Jim, on his part, intuitively feels that Brown and his men are "the emissaries with whom the world he had renounced was pursuing him in his retreat."

Perceiving the potential menace of Brown and his "rapacious" white followers, Jim approaches the entire situation with caution; he knows that there will be either "a clear road or else a clear fight" ahead. His one thought, as he informs Doramin, is "for the people's good." Preparations for battle now take place around the fort, and the feeling among the natives is one of anxiety, and also of hope that Jim will somehow resolve everything by convincing Brown that the way back to the sea would be a peaceful one. Jim is convinced "that it would be best to let these whites and their followers go with their lives." Unwavering as always in meeting his moral obligations, he is primarily concerned with the safety of Patusan. But he underestimates the calculating Brown, again disclosing the propensity that betrays him. Quite simply Jim does not mistrust Brown, believing as he does that both of them want to avoid bloodshed. In this respect, illusion both comforts and victimizes Jim, as the way is made clear for Brown, with the sniveling Cornelius at his side providing him with directions, to withdraw from Patusan, now guarded by Dain Waris's forces.

Brown's purpose is not only to escape but also to get even with Jim for not becoming his ally, and to punish the natives for their earlier resistance to his intrusion. When retreating towards the coast his men deceitfully open fire on an outpost of Patusan, killing the surprised and panic-striken natives, as well as Dain Waris, "the only son of Nakhoda Doramin," who had earlier acceded to Jim's request that Brown and his party should be allowed to leave without harm. It could have been otherwise, to be sure, given the superior numbers of the native defenders. Once again, it is made painfully clear, Jim flinches in discernment and in leadership, naively trusting in his illusion, in his dream, unaware of the evil power of retribution that impels Brown and that slinks in humankind. That, too, Brown's schooner later sprung a bad leak and sank, he himself being the only survivor to be found in a white longboat, and that the deceitful Cornelius was to be found and struck down by Jim's ever-loyal servant, Tamb' Itam, can hardly compensate for the destruction and the deaths that took place as a result of Jim's failure of judgment. Marlow's earlier demurring remark has a special relevance at this point: "I would have trusted the deck to that youngster [Jim] on the strength of a single glance . . . but, by Jove! it wouldn't have been safe."

Jim's decision to allow free passage to Brown stems from his concern with preserving an orderly community in Patusan: he did not want to see all his good work and influence destroyed by violent acts. But clearly he had misjudged Brown's character. Neither Jim's honesty nor his courage, however, are to be impugned; his moral sense, in this case, is what consciously guided his rational conception of civilization. But a failure of moral vision, induced perhaps by moral pride and romanticism, blinds him to real danger. When Tamb' Itam returns from the outpost to inform Jim about what has happened, Jim is staggered. He fathoms fully the effects of Brown's "cruel treachery," even as he understands that his own safety in Patusan is now at risk, given Dain Waris's death and Doramin's dismay and grief over events for which he holds Jim responsible. For Jim the entire situation is untenable, as well as perplexing: "He had retreated from one world for a small matter of an impulsive jump, and now the other, the work of his own hands, had fallen in ruins upon his head." His feeling of isolation is rending, as he realizes that "he has lost again all men's confidence." The "Dark Powers" have robbed him twice of his peace.

To Tamb' Itam's plea that he should fight for his life against Doramin's inevitable revenge, Jim bluntly cries, "I have no life." Jewel, too, "wrestling with him for the possession of her happiness," also begs him to put up a fight, or try to escape, but Jim does not heed her. "He was going to prove his power in another way and conquer the fatal destiny itself." This is, truly, "a day of evil, an accursed day," for Jim and for Patusan. When Dain Waris's body is brought into Doramin's *campong*, the "old *nakhoda*" was "to let out one great fierce cry . . . as mighty as the bellow of a wounded bull." The scene here is harrowing in terms of grief, as the women of the household "began to wail together; they mourned with shrill cries; the sun was setting, and in the intervals of screamed lamentations the high singsong voices of two old men intoning the Koran chanted alone." The scene is desolate, unconsoling, rendered in the language of apocalypse; the sky over Patusan is blood red, with "an enormous sun nestled crimson amongst the treetops, and the forest below had a black and forbidding face." Jim now appears silently before Doramin, who is sitting in his armchair, a pair of flintlock pistols on his knees. "I am come in sorrow," he cries out to Doramin, who stares at Jim "with an expression of mad pain, of rage, with a ferocious glitter. . . . and lifting deliberately his right [hand], shot his son's friend through the chest."

At the end of his explanatory letter Marlow remarks that Jim "passes away under a cloud, inscrutable at heart, forgotten, unforgiven, and excessively romantic." Such a remark, of course, must be placed in the context of Marlow's total narrative, with all of the tensions and the ambiguities that occur in relating the story of Jim's life as it unfolds in the novel. Nor can Marlow's words here be construed as a moral censure of Jim. What exemplifies Marlow's narrative, in fact, is the integrity of its content, as the details, reflections, judgments, demurrals emerge with astonishing and attenuating openness, deliberation. There is no single aspect of Jim's life and character that is not measured and presented in full view of the reader. If judgment is to be made regarding Jim's situation, Conrad clearly shows, then affirmations and doubts, triumphs and failures, will have to be disclosed and evaluated cumulatively.

No one is more mercilessly exposed to the world than Jim. And no one stands more naked before our judgment than he. The scrutiny of Jim's beliefs and attitudes, and of his actions and inactions, is relentless in depth and latitude. He himself cannot hide or flee, no matter where he happens to be. Marlow well discerns Jim's supreme aloneness in his struggles to find himself in himself, to master his fate, beyond the calumnies of his enemies and the loyalty and love of his friends—and beyond his own rigorous self-judgments. The anguish of Jim's struggle consumes everything and everyone in the novel, and nothing and no one can be the same again once in contact with him. In Jim, it can be said, we see ourselves, for he is "one of us," he is our "common fate," which prohibits us to "let him slip away into the darkness."

From a moral perspective the Official Court of Inquiry literally takes place throughout *Lord Jim*. Jim never ceases to react to charges of cowardice and of irresponsibility; never ceases to strive earnestly to prove his moral worthiness. He seems never to be in a state of repose, is always under pressure, always examining his tensive state of mind and soul. Self-illumination rather than self-justification, or even self-rehabilitation, is his central aim, and he knows, too, that such a process molds his own efforts and pain. He neither expects nor accepts help or absolution from others, nor does he blame others for his own sins of commission or omission. His character is thus one of singular transparency, acutely self-conscious, and vulnerable.

Jim's moral sense weighs heavily on him and drives him on sundry, sometimes contradictory, lines of moral awareness and behavior. In this respect he brings to mind the relevance of Edmund Burke's words: "The lines of morality are not like the ideal lines of mathematics. They are broad and deep as well as long. They admit of exceptions; they demand modifications."[4] Gnostic commentators who view the moral demands of this novel as confusing or uncertain fail to see that the lines of morality, even when they take different directions and assume different forms, inevitably crystallize in something that is solid in revelation and in value.[5]

Clearly Jim's high-mindedness and character are problematic, and his scale of human values is excessively romantic. Thus he romanticizes what it means to be a sailor, what duty is, even what cowardice is. The fact is that he is too "noble" to accommodate real-life situations. In essence, then, Jim violates what the ancient Greeks revered as the "law of measure." And

---

[4]*The Philosophy of Edmund Burke. A Selection from His Speeches and Writings*, edited and with an Introduction by Louis I. Bredvold and Ralph G. Ross (Ann Arbor MI, 1960) 41.

[5]See, for example, Douglas Hewitt, "Lord Jim," in *Conrad: A Reassessment* (Chester Springs PA, 1969) 31-39.

ultimately his pride, his lofty conception of what is required of him in terms of responsible leadership and duty, his high idealism mar the supreme Hellenic virtue of sophrosynē. Jim's conduct dramatizes to an "unsafe" degree the extremes of arrogance, and of self-delusion and self-assertion. Above all his idealism becomes a peculiar kind of escape from the paradoxes and antinomies that have to be faced in what Burke calls the "antagonist world."

In the end, Jim's habit of detachment and abstraction manifestly rarefies his moral sense and diminishes and even neutralizes the moral meaning of his decisions and actions. His self-proclaimed autonomy dramatizes monomania and egoism, and makes him incapable of harmonious human interrelations, let alone a redeeming humility. His moral sense is consequently incomplete as a paradigm, and his moral virtues are finite. And his fate, as it is defined and shaped by his tragic flaw, does not attain true grandeur. In Jim, it can be said, Conrad presents heroism with all its limitations.[6]

Despite the circumstances of his moral incompleteness, Jim both possesses and enacts the quality of endurance in facing the darkness in himself and in the world around him. Even when he yearns to conceal himself in some forgotten corner of the universe, there to separate himself from other imperfect or fallen humans, from thieves and renegades, and from the harsh exigencies of existence, he also knows that unconditional separation is not attainable. He persists, however erratically or skeptically, in his pursuit to reconcile the order of the community and the order of the soul; and he perseveres in his belief in the axiomatic principles of honor, of loyalty, prescribing the need to transcend inner and outer moral squalor. His death, even if it shows the power of violence, of the evil that stalks man and humanity, of the flaws and foibles that afflict one's self, does not diminish the abiding example of Jim's struggle to discover and to overcome moral lapses.

Jim can never silence the indwelling moral sense which inspires and illuminates his life-journey. Throughout this journey the virtue of endurance does not abandon him, does not betray him, even when he betrays himself and others. He endures in order to prevail. In *Lord Jim*, Joseph

---

[6]My explication of the ideas found in this and the preceding paragraph owes much to Professor Claes G. Ryn's discerning and detailed critique of my appraisal of *Lord Jim*, as found in his letter to me dated March 4, 2000.

Conrad portrays a fitful but ascendant process of transfiguration in the life of a solitary hero whose courage of endurance contains the seeds of redemption. Such a life recalls the eternal promise of the Evangelist's words: "He that endureth to the end shall be saved."[7]

[7]Matthew 10:22.

Chapter 3

Victory

I

Can a man of moral sensitivity function in a corrupt and derelict world? This is a major question that Joseph Conrad probes in *Victory* (1915) and that his main character, Axel Heyst, presumably a Swedish baron, depicts through a demanding process of self-examination and self-discovery. Conrad, to be sure, conveys in this novel the fundamental pessimism and melancholy that stamp his view of the human condition. But at the same time, he also shows how the power of redemption unfolds in the decisions and the actions which Heyst strenuously enacts in the course of the novel's happenings. In him we see a deep, agonizing struggle going on between his habit of detachment and his instinctive need to involve himself in the life-process as he tears his self away from the doubts and fears which prevent one from putting trust in life. As Heyst moves out of his self-chosen isolation on the island of Samburan in the Malaysian Archipelago, he asserts faith in the essential meaning and dignity of the human being. He personifies precisely what Henry James calls the "emotion of recognition" as he collides with the power of the world, and finds that he cannot kill the invisible God within him.

With Shakespeare's Prince Hamlet, Conrad's "Hamlet of the South Seas" sees this world as "an unweeded garden / That grows to seed; things rank and gross in nature / Possess it merely."[1] Heyst's worldview is rooted in despair, which impels him to choose the isolation that, in the end, transforms into "sickness unto death." "Heyst was not conscious of either friends or of enemies," Conrad writes. "It was the very essence of his life to be a solitary achievement, accomplished not by hermit-like withdrawal with its silence and immobility, but by a system of restless wandering, by the detachment of an impermanent dweller amongst changing scenes." In short, Heyst seeks to become "invulnerable because elusive." *Victory*

---

[1]This particular reference to *Hamlet*, act I, scene II, lines 141-43, was drawn to my attention by Frederick R. Karl's *A Reader's Guide to Joseph Conrad* (New York, 1969) 246.

renders the full costs of an attitude rooted in cynical and selfish indifference—to hide, to abstain, to do nothing.

The structure and the thrust of this novel, in their organic interaction, delineate the unceasing tugs and turns of Heyst's efforts. Even the sudden time shifts and truncations in the novel's structure heighten the furious strains and dissonance besieging Heyst. In this respect *Victory* can be seen as a novel of multiplying tensions, in terms of space and time, as we view Heyst struggling to free himself from the influence of his late father, an expatriated Swedish philosopher of disenchantment, with whom the young Heyst, having now left school, lived in London: "Three years of such companionship at that plastic and impressionable age were bound to leave in the boy a profound distrust of life." The elder Heyst, "dissatisfied with his [own] country and angry with all the world," had grimly concluded that mankind was no longer worthy of the right to moral and intellectual freedom. His final advice to his son was "to cultivate that form of contempt which is called pity," to "Look on and never make a sound," for "he who forms a tie is lost"—"the last words of the man who had spent his life in blowing blasts upon a terrible trumpet which had filled heaven and earth with ruins, while mankind went on its way unheeding."

Following the death of his father, and for a period of fifteen years thereafter, Heyst made distant travels "in unexplored countries, in the wilds," as he proceeded to organize his life in accordance with his father's vision of existence. Heyst seeks to confirm his father's basic belief that "The world is a bad dog. It will bite you if you give it a chance. . . . " Darkness and ominous silences become Heyst's companions in his enterprise to make his life "a masterpiece of aloofness." He chooses to work as manager for the Tropical Belt Coal Company, which is located on Samburan ("the 'Round Island' of the charts") and remain there even after the firm has gone into liquidation. Here Heyst "was out of everybody's way, as if he were perched on the highest peak of the Himalayas." And here, except for aimless visits to neighboring islands, he remained unconnected and disconnected—still removed from the flow of life and still the dutiful son (at the age of thirty-five) of the "destroyer of systems, of hopes, of beliefs."

Heyst agonizes over a yearning to "drift" and an instinct to "plunge," thereby to make a moral commitment to humankind. "No decent feeling was ever spurned by Heyst," Conrad's omniscient narrator observes. In him a peculiar transparency and sincerity are dominant. However much Heyst wants to avoid human contact, insofar as "all action is bound to be harmful," he cannot consciously ignore a "distressed humanity." Nor can his "seclusion in his lost corner of the Eastern seas" keep him from responding to calls for help. As the narrator reminds us, Heyst was not one who "paused" much once his heart and conscience spoke to him: "Those dreamy spectators of the world's agitation are terrible once the desire to act gets hold of them. They lower their heads and charge a wall with an amazing serenity which nothing but an indisciplined imagination can give."

In Heyst we discern how a man of "universal detachment" transforms into a man of moral action. In effect, Heyst resists the "sin" that is despair, which pollutes the soul. But more than anything else he surmounts his craving for abstraction as he answers the appeals made to him by human beings threatened with being crushed under the iron heel of some sinister life force. Heyst discloses quiet, firm courage once he ventures out of the prison house of "pernicious reflecton." Clearly Heyst's detachment was not complete—"And incompleteness of any sort leads to trouble." In the end he personifies the truth of words spoken by one of Conrad's later admirers, Albert Camus: "The individual can do nothing and yet he can do everything."

The first to call on Heyst's innate humanity is Morrison, the owner and master of a trading brig, whose acts of generosity to natives barely subsisting in a "quantity of God-forsaken villages up dark creeks and obscure bays," lead to his economic misfortune. The two men chance to meet on the island of Timor, at a pestilential town called Delli. At the time Morrison, an Englishman from Dorsetshire, was in serious trouble with the Portuguese authorities, who, claiming an irregularity in his papers, had taken his brig, which they planned to auction unless he paid a specified fine. Without any spare cash in hand, Morrison faces ruin. His state of desperation deeply moves Heyst, who formally and politely pays the fine and thus saves Morrison from ruin. He discerns in Morrison an honest and honorable man, the victim of too many altruisms. Clearly the virtues in Morrison's character arouse Heyst's sympathy. The decision to help Morrison initiates both a change in Heyst and a redirection of his moral conversion, as he begins to discern the hollow man in himself.

A thankful Morrison views Heyst's help as miraculous—" 'Miracles do happen,' thought the awestruck Morrison. . . . The fact of his turning up in Timor or anywhere else was no more wonderful than the settling of a sparrow on one's windowsill at any given moment." But the impecunious Morrison also knows that he will never be able to repay "this amazing emissary of Providence." Hence he invites the Swede to travel with him in his brig and to share in his trading enterprises in the Archipelago. Heyst accepts Morrison's invitation, if only to put an end to their mutual embarrassment that springs from a common personal reserve. This arrangement in the end resulted in Heyst becoming the manager of the Tropical Belt Coal Company in the tropics, the original idea of which Morrison himself had pushed for successfully when he returned to London. But Morrison himself does not survive, as Conrad's narrator informs us: "the victim of gratitude and his native climate, [he] had gone to join his forefathers in a Dorsetshire churchyard." Heyst selected Samburan to be the central station, but the mining venture eventually failed, and he himself "faded completely away." It was months later that Captain Davidson, a delicate and humane man, coming from the westward in his steamer the *Sissie*, saw him with his own eyes: "he made out with his glass the white figure on the coaling wharf. . . . He looked exactly as we have always seen him—very neat, white shoes, cork helmet."

If the encounter with Morrison does not lead to Heyst's worldly enrichment, it does have a deep and lasting effect on his inner self. It is because of Morrison's plight that Heyst forms a tie with another human being, and it is also because of Morrison that he brings to the surface his feelings of humanity, to which he consciously submits. Morrison prods Heyst's faculty of conscience, which is synonymous with the inward knowledge and inmost thought that are part of the mental system. But, above all, in Heyst conscience serves as an intimate function of the moral sense in the discernment of right and wrong. It is what enables him to begin the process of unmasking the deformed titanism of his father's philosophy. Conscience is Heyst's interior strength, pregnant with the moral possibilities that he visibilizes in his life after Morrison. Morrison, as such, signifies the emergence of the first of Heyst's affirmations in the form of an ascending moral courage.

The second call on Heyst for help has momentous consequences for himself and for others with whom he has made connections. The novel renders these consequences with a relentless inevitability. Having first established a human tie with Morrison, Heyst had exposed himself to his humanity and thus made himself vulnerable to the kind of fatal outcome his father foresaw. This second call speaks to his passional self, to his heart. There is no turning back for him once he listens to what his heart tells him to do, introducing as it does a new and dangerous dynamic in his life. He can never be the same after he makes another "plunge," this time in the course of reappearing in European-ruled nearby Sourabaya, having earlier signalled Captain Davidson to take him there. Here he stays at a hotel owned by a German, Schomberg, who detested and regularly maligned

Heyst. Schomberg's was an instinctive hatred for "a genuine gentleman" whose aloofness and independence rankled the hotelkeeper. Such hatred has its origin in diabolism, with which Heyst will have to contend mightily in due course.

At Schomberg's hotel, as it happens, a ladies' orchestra ("Zangiacomo's eastern tour—eighteen performers") is giving evening concerts. The Zangiacomos are hardly musicians by profession. Among the performers is found a twenty-year-old English girl, Lena. Heyst visits the concert hall, where he is immediately assaulted by the coarseness of the scene: "An instrumental uproar, screaming, grunting, whining, sobbing, scraping, squeaking some kind of lively air; while a grand piano operated upon by a bony red-faced woman with bad-tempered nostrils rained hard notes like hail through the tempest of fiddles." The sordidness of this scene—"something cruel, sensual and repulsive"—strikes Heyst as "awful," "incorrect." He feels pity for the performers, whom he views as "exploited, hopeless, devoid of charm and grace." The same kind of humane impulse that prompted him earlier to reach out to Morrison again takes hold of Heyst when he observes Lena being cruelly pinched (not for the first time) by another performer. In Lena he perceives a forsaken and affronted human being whose situation fills him with moral outrage.

Heyst's compassion for Lena's suffering and humiliation—she is also called Alma and Magdalene—leads him, after another visit to the concert hall, to assure her that he will take her away from the Zangiacomos, as well as from sexual predators like Schomberg. His moral outrage is now touched by deep stirrings in his heart. Lena has a mysterious, mesmerizing effect on Heyst, who seems captured by the fineness of her features, by her seductive voice, by an "immense sadness" that surrounds her like a halo, by her air of innocence. "He could not defend himself from compassion." For her, too, Heyst himself is like some savior whose kindness and sincerity fill her with admiration. This new encounter between Heyst and Lena is both electrifying and redemptive, as two human beings, a savior and a victim, plod their way to a tragic freedom. Lena enables Heyst to attain his second major affirmation.

Yet, too, if Heyst is aware of her circumstances, and seeks to save her, he is also aware of the dangers and costs. In him the man of reflection wrestles incessantly with the man of compassion, for he is still assailed by the doubts and fears implanted in him by his famous philosopher-father. But in the end "his sceptical mind was dominated by the fulness of his heart." The drama of their nocturnal escape gains in a momentum that blends moral responsibility and passional feelings. Lena at this point is a "white, phantom-like apparition," as they both cling to each other in the face of a hostile world.

Conrad renders the entire episode with astonishing power, as two human beings, with the secret help of Schomberg's pitiably abused wife, defy the terror and treachery of a world that they have come to distrust and fear, embodied in Schomberg's hotel, which can be likened to a subterranean realm of vice and oppressive cruelties and calumnies. Heyst can hardly ignore Lena's desperate plea for his help in escaping from diabolic forces. He must take her away, she begs, for he is her only hope: "You told me you had always been alone, you had never had a dog even. Well, then, I won't be in anybody's way if I live with you—not even a dog's." The pathos of her position nearly overwhelms him as he grasps just how vulnerable she is: "He put his arms around her, and only by the convulsive movements of her body became aware that she was sobbing without a sound. Sustaining her, he lost himself in the profound silence of the night." Their stealthy escape to "the solitude of Samburan," when it is finally executed, underlines Heyst's "departure from the part of an unconcerned spectator." But that "departure" does not necessarily insure absolute safety; indeed, it marks still another of the "incalculable consequences" once "the germ of corruption" has entered the soul.

Life on Samburan is far from easy for either Heyst or Lena. It seems that the furies are still chasing them during the more than three months since their flight from Sourabaya. The memory of Morrison haunts Heyst in his view of "this earthly captivity" in which "cornered" human beings like Lena must struggle to overcome somehow. "There is something of my father in every man who lives long enough," he asserts at one point to Lena, and goes on to say, "Man on this earth is an unforeseen accident which does not stand close investigation." Nor does Heyst's memory of his father lessen as he seeks to explain to Lena the paradox of human existence: "Suppose the world were a factory and all mankind workmen in it," he further asserts. "Well, he [the elder Heyst] discovered that the wages were not good enough. That they were paid in counterfeit money." It seems, too, that the man with the quill pen in his hand, as found in the oil portrait of his father that he retains in his bungalow in Samburan, is always looking down at Heyst, as if to remind him of the snares of making a commitment to other human beings in a world that is nothing more than "storm and dust" (the title of one of his father's many books). In Heyst, Conrad portrays schisms of the soul and lacerations of thought that buffet him in his decisions. The movement, if not the form, of the novel itself mirrors the internal solipsisms that wrack Heyst, and the polarizing doubts and denials that shake his mind and soul.

To the very end Heyst fights a running battle with "his conception of a world not worth touching, and perhaps not substantial enough to grasp." His relationship with Lena reflects the grip of this conception. Their long conversations help the reader to acquire a clearer understanding of Heyst's earlier life, attitudes, reactions, and thus piece together a more coherent picture of Heyst's thinking and conduct, even in his silences. His inward terrain, as it were, becomes better known to the reader. With Lena, Heyst has discovered human communion. But at the same time there lingered in him an incompleteness that he would never overcome—"the fatal imperfections of all the gifts of life, which makes of them a delusion and a snare." His confessions to her have a way of marking her as a saintly figure, pure in her innocence and suffering, one who (Heyst thinks aloud in his mind) "had a special grace in the intimacy of life." Lena enables us to penetrate what one critic calls "the patterns of self-division" in Heyst,[2] whose greatest difficulty is in relating to another human being, to what D. H. Lawrence calls "divine otherness." Lena helps Heyst to gain a keener sense of his own reality, and thus to advance beyond his self-division. But his incompleteness is never fully healed, and he cannot openly admit his love for Lena, even when he has demonstrated passion for her: "He swerved and, stepping up to her, sank to the ground by her side. . . . he took her in his arms and kissed her lips. He tasted on them the bitterness of a tear fallen there. He had never seen her cry. It was like another appeal to his tenderness—a new seduction."

Although he frowned on F. M. Dostoevsky, Conrad fully grasped the meaning of the Russian novelist's belief that, in the human soul, good and evil are forever struggling. No one, as Heyst himself discovers, escapes the ferocity of such a struggle. One may want to avoid it, or to sublimate it, or refuse to recognize it, but one can never absolutely deny its existence. And one can have absolutely no illusion about the terrors of its might. The failure to recognize evil constitutes a moral lapse; and the failure to resist it leads to moral lassitude, if not to moral death itself. To neutralize evil is

---

[2]Here I am indebted to H. M. Daleski, "*Victory* and Patterns of Self-Division," in *Conrad Revisited: Essays for the Eighties*, ed. Ross C. Murfin (Tuscaloosa AL, 1985) 107-23.

an impossibility, for it will make itself known to one without warning, within and yet beyond temporal and spatial entities. It will invade any refuge and break down any wall built to keep out its infernal energies.

In Schomberg we are in contact with one of Nietzsche's "great despisers." "He works with immense malice." His is an inborn detestation of the good, which he will undermine in any manner he can. Schomberg will say anything to anyone at anytime for the purpose of defaming Heyst. Thus he spreads rumors that Heyst is Morrison's murderer, that as the latter's partner he got all he could out of him and then sent him away to die. He compares Heyst to a spider: "Don't you ever get caught in his web." No less vicious are Schomberg's stories about Heyst as Lena's seducer. The Liar, a name for Satan, finds a loyal follower in Wilhelm Schomberg.

II

In his composite of evil Conrad presents a graphic picture of "Satan in our day."[3] His devils are bent on the destruction of life and spirit, and of all norms of law and morals. They ultimately force Heyst to move closer to reality, further distancing him from the terrible illusions, the abstractions of flight and detachment, which the elder Heyst concocted as protection against any involvement in the life-process. In Conrad's metaphysics of evil we observe how theory and reality collide with a violent crash, as this collision is etched in Heyst's life. Heyst, it is clear, cannot run away from either himself or life around him; nor can he run away from the fact of evil itself, whether it is found in the world or in himself. Evil, as we observe it in *Victory*, constitutes a complete and inclusive attack on the order of life and the order of the soul. It is the moral and not the theological dimension of evil that Conrad mainly confronts in this novel. Evil embodies moral disorder, and its afflictions are multifarious. Conrad's devils appear like dreadful diseases, odious in nature, dismal, deformed, bestial, snarling.[4] For

---

[3]Perhaps one of the finest books on the subject of demonology is *Satan*, ed. Père Bruno de Jesus-Marie, with an introduction by Charles Moeller (New York, 1951). This remarkable collection of essays, written by various theologians and scholars, deals with "Satan's Existence and Nature"; "The Place of the Devil Outside Christianity"; "Possession and Diabolism"; "The Devil in Art and Literature"; and "Deicide."

[4]See Stanton de Voren Hoffman's suggestive essay, "Conrad's Menagerie: Animal Imagery and Theme," *Bucknell Review* (December 1964): 59-71.

them, in Conrad's words, it is "as if the world were still one great, wild jungle without law." These "unclean spirits" stop at nothing in creating chaos; they are like wild beasts prowling in the ruins of a maritime Nineveh.

The "human satans" in *Victory* are Mr. Jones, Martin Ricardo, and Pedro. They arrive in Sourabaya "one fine morning," coming "from up China Sea way." They are greeted by Schomberg on his steam-launch, which he used for boarding arriving passenger ships in his search for "promising accounts." One of the trio, Mr. Jones, immediately hails Schomberg by name, knowing of him and his illicit reputation. The hotel-keeper views them as "desperadoes," but he wants to exploit them for his own devious purposes. In the presence of all four of them we detect their common recognition of each other's demonic energies. Each of them adheres to an agenda for evil, and each one projects particular physical attributes that are in keeping with one's demonism. These attributes add to the mystery of their evil in its parts and in its whole. Conrad is clearly making the point that the new "guests" staying in Schomberg's hotel are as morally reprehensible as they are physically grotesque. From the moment they are introduced, Conrad is preparing the reader for a spectacle of devils and, more specifically, for the moral and spiritual battle that will ensue. They are in and of the world, as they "walketh about" seeking whom to devour;[5] they are in time and yet beyond time, and they come from everywhere and are everywhere.

In *Victory* Conrad goes to great length to picture the physical elements of evil. "Plain Mr. Jones," Martin Ricardo, and Pedro bring to mind "the infernal Proteus," that is, the diabolical antitrinity of the Book of Revelation: the False Prophet, the Dragon, and the Beast. In Conrad's three demoniacs we have an equivalent androgynous animality, shorn of any semblance of spirituality. Even the hotelkeeper is impressed by the spirit of evil his guests emanate: "Schomberg, raising his eyes at last, met the gleams in two dark caverns under Mr. Jones's devilish eyebrows, directed upon him impenetrably. He shuddered as if horrors worse than murder had been lurking there. . . . " Mr. Jones, the supreme "outlaw," has an emaciated, clean-shaven face, a long and loose-jointed body, sunken eyes, long, feminine, beautifully pencilled eyelashes, which give him "a used-up, weary, depraved distinction," with an "air of withered youth." Subject to

---

[5]First Peter 5:8.

fits, he has a spectral presence which strikes terror in those he addresses in a voice that is "indifferent, as if issuing from a tomb."

Mr. Jone's "secretary," "the equivocal Ricardo," is a short, muscular man, whose eyes gleam and blink; he has "a harsh voice, and a round, toneless, pockmarked face ornamented by a thin, dishevelled moustache," which sticks out "under the tip of a rigid nose." He seems only too anxious to pounce on another person "with teeth and claws," or to set fire to a house without the slightest delay. He has the expression of "a cat which sees a piece of fish in the pantry out of reach"; and he is "game for anything from pitch and toss to wilful murder." To Ricardo, then, "life was not a matter of passive renunciation, but of a particularly active warfare."

Between Mr. Jones and Ricardo, the narrator points out, there existed "a similarity of mind"—"one the outcast of his vices, the other inspired by a spirit of scornful defiance." It can be said that Ricardo has always been waiting for Mr. Jones, in whom his corrupt nature finds its consummation. While serving as a mate on a schooner plying the waters in the Gulf of Mexico, Ricardo met Mr. Jones, instinctively choosing "to follow him," for "he seemed to touch me inside somewhere." From that first meeting, and now continuing for more than four years, "Mr. Secretary Ricardo," "simple—and faithful—and wonderfully acute," has been carrying out Mr. Jones's commands with utmost obedience.

The last of the trio, Pedro, an alligator hunter from Colombia, is a "nondescript, hairy creature" who seems to tag after the other two, and who is obviously useful to their purposes. Conrad endows him with all the characteristics of an anthropoidal type who belongs to a "shaggy, hair-smothered humanity." Pedro, unlike the other two, represents the simple, straightforward brutality of evil; he does not have their "subtle power of terror." We learn from Ricardo that Pedro first joined the thieving pair in Nicaragua, where Mr. Jones and Ricardo had found lodgings in the hut of Pedro and his brother, Antonio. The brothers were in the meanwhile scheming to murder Mr. Jones and Ricardo and rob them of the booty they had acquired during their various treasure-hunting expeditions in the Gulf of Mexico. Ricardo, detecting the motives of the two brothers, informs Mr. Jones, who instantly "plugs a bullet plumb centre into Mr. Antonio's chest." The killing, carried out one night with conscienceless alacrity, reveals Mr. Jones's diabolical disposition of mind and movement. Pedro, once he is subdued (with some difficulty) by Ricardo, after attempting to escape, has his life spared by Mr. Jones. And since that time a grateful Pedro attached himself to Mr. Jones. The evil alliance of Mr. Jones,

Ricardo, and Pedro was thus to arise from infernal circumstances that knit together "a spectre, a cat, an ape."

After several weeks have passed, Mr. Jones and his henchmen still remain in the hotel, practically appropriating it for their "discreet operations with cards." Anxious to be rid of his three guests, and to regain his business from the oppression of "thieves, gamblers, and murderers," Schomberg decides to put Ricardo "on another track": he tells him of Heyst and the "plunder" he has hidden on Samburan. The story fascinates Ricardo, particularly the part on Lena. Schomberg manipulates the various details in enticing and devious ways, not only to free himself of the trio but also to get back at Heyst, whom he blames for taking Lena away from him. The conversation between the two discloses a mutual diabolism, as one man of evil plays with another man of evil. One must not underestimate the depth of Schomberg's own diabolism, as he seeks to outmaneuver Ricardo, to steer him to new heights of evil by doing Schomberg's dirty work against Heyst. His cunning is subtle in development as he draws for Ricardo the way to Samburan. "For people like you," he says to Ricardo, "three days in a good, big boat is nothing. It's no more than a little outing, a bit of a change."

Schomberg's "expressive combination of words" has a deep effect on Ricardo, who is anxious for a new skirmish on a new front. All he needs is a little imaginative prodding from Schomberg. There is a kind of sparring going on between them, with Schomberg having the upper hand as he is driven by his monomania to destroy Heyst as the cause of his "ruined hopes." He thus persuades Ricardo, who is ready "to get his claws out at any moment," to "proceed with the business." (Schomberg will even provide the trio with a boat and provisions, as well as with courses and charts.) Mr. Jones, as Ricardo also reveals, "funks facing women," preferring instead the occasional company of "a ragged, barelegged boy," and therefore he simply will say nothing about Lena to the "governor." For the hotel-keeper this is a moment of great strategic importance: "Schomberg's heart began to thump as he saw himself nearing his vengeance." And for Heyst, who has "never killed a man or loved a woman," a fatal battle on Samburan looms when he first sights a big boat with three men at the wharf, under the jetty—"envoys of the outer world. . . . evil intelligence, instinctive savagery, arm in arm. The brute force is at the back."

With this "visitation" comes the last stage of visible and invisible warfare on the island of Samburan and in the soul of Axel Heyst. He looks on this visitation as one "of a particularly offensive kind," and he is intuitively aware of the dire consequences now that "the outer world had broken upon him." A prowling Ricardo carefully surveys the surroundings, and is anxious to find the exact location of Heyst's treasure. Conrad shrouds the entire scene in mystery and danger. Wang, a Chinese servant who, with his Alfuro wife, lived in a hut near Heyst, purloins Heyst's revolver and later runs away from the immediate area surrounding three bungalows, fearing that Heyst is doomed by the three visitors. Conrad creates here an atmosphere of fatality. For Heyst the test of his courage, of his affection for Lena, and above all of his moral will, is close at hand. But will he be able to cast out the devils, as it were, when the appointed time comes? This is a major question that emerges in the concluding scenes in *Victory*.

Heyst is at the epicenter of the novel's happenings at this point, and we observe him from different angles. What he has always feared to contend with, that is, "the embodied evil of the world," now comes to knock at the door of his soul. All the tensions of his "yes" and "no" converge in the form of diabolisms seeking his destruction. In this final movement of the novel, Heyst comes to see his past and present breaking in on him, recognizing fully, as he does, that "I have lived too long within myself, watching the mere shadows and shades of life." The moral questions that *Victory* raises crystallize in this omega-point of the novel.

III

The mood in these last events (in part IV) is grim, and one feels their intensity and turbulence. Light seems to slide into darkness with no warning, and darkness itself suddently manifests flashes of lightning, punctuated by thunder, followed by a brooding silence. A nervous confusion seems to prevail, as we see Ricardo scurrying here and there—hiding, watching, stalking, skulking, dodging. At one point, Ricardo enters Heyst's house while the latter is in discourse with Mr. Jones in another bungalow. There he discovers Lena, "her fingers busy with her dark hair, utterly unconscious, exposed and defenceless and tempting. . . . The instinct for the feral spring could no longer be denied." He attacks Lena, who resists him fiercely and successfully with exceptional strength that comes from her devotion to Heyst. Ricardo is all amazement and wonder; to him, she is a "blooming miracle," and he now confides in her his passional feelings and also his plans to rob (and, if necessary, kill) Heyst.

Lena senses the full danger that faces the man who saved her, and now resorts to duplicity in handling Ricardo, who still believes Schomberg's story that Heyst had abducted her. Now that Ricardo has told her about the scheme against Heyst, she is more determined than ever to save the man she loves. Ricardo, infatuated with Lena, deludes himself in believing he has "intelligences in the enemy's camp." Quietly Ricardo begins to distance himself from Mr. Jones: "He no longer felt comfortable alone with the governor." Lena has entered Ricardo's life with a vengeance, and she will use him any way she can to protect Heyst.

Fully perceptive of the dangers that "the envoys extraordinary of the world" pose, Heyst fears for Lena's safety. But Heyst has self-doubts about whether or not he can stand up to the "evil men." Unarmed and desperate, he tries to think of ways of escaping with Lena, but these come to nought. While wandering with Heyst in the forest, Lena intuits "a sullen, dumb, menacing hostility," and she "feels the nearness of death." A feeling of doom also inheres in Heyst's inner thoughts, as he thinks of Lena: "He regretted that he had no Heaven, to which he could recommend this fair, palpitating handful of ashes and dust. . . . " His fears are heightened by "the ill-omened chaos of the sky," again reminding us of Conrad's astonishing way of interfusing human life and the natural elements, at a point when a wild storm is about to erupt at an "evil hour."

Heyst and Mr. Jones are the great antagonists in the final pages of *Victory*; they confront each other fatefully in a time of "reckoning." Mr. Jones believes that Heyst has "no stomach for a fight," while he himself is "the retribution that waits its time." But increasingly Heyst does become aware he is dealing with "an absolutely hard and pitiless scoundrel." They speak to each other as opposing equals in intelligence. When Heyst reveals to him that Lena was in fact living with him on the island, Mr. Jones is quick to gauge the meaning of Ricardo's infidelity. In the midst of all this, Heyst suddenly sees Lena, dressed in black, sitting "enthroned" in a chair, beyond the door in the candle-lit room of his bungalow. (She did not flee to the safety of the forest, as he had instructed her earlier.) Seated nearby on the floor is Ricardo, gazing at Lena with "the absorbed, all-forgetful rapture of his contemplation."

Death is now in the air—the death that Lena sees is preparing to capture Heyst. Her sole purpose is how to get hold of Ricardo's knife. She is able to deceive Ricardo, and even manages to have him give her the knife. Ricardo now creeps closer to Lena, clasping her ankle and kissing the instep. As she pushes him away with a violence, he begins to realize the extent of her duplicity and leaps to his feet, as he also hears "the brief report of a shot" that grazes Ricardo's head. It was Mr. Jones who fired the shot over Heyst's shoulder, we learn. Entering the house, Heyst looks concernedly at Lena, who appears triumphant since she believes she has successfully saved him from Ricardo. Heyst, with Davidson by his side—coincidentally the latter has just arrived—picks up Lena's limp body from the chair, and places her on the bed in the other room. There they find that the bullet Mr. Jones fired had entered under Lena's breast. It is a dying Lena we behold here, yet a Lena who has achieved "victory over death" by saving Heyst. He, however, somehow seems unable to take her into his arms and carry her out of "this lonely place": "Heyst bent low over her, cursing his fastidious soul, which even at that moment kept the true cry of love from his lips in its infernal distrust of all life. He dared not touch her, and she had no longer the strength to throw her arms about his neck."

From his candid testimony to an inquiring high official, we learn that what prompted Davidson to go ashore, at the very point of Lena's death, was his discovery of a big white boat, with the dead body of Pedro inside, bumping against the bow of his steamer. We also learn from Davidson that Mr. Jones had fatally shot Ricardo, and that Wang, out of pity and curiosity, having followed Heyst and Lena through the forest, had shot a dozing Pedro in the boat. He then cut the boat adrift, fearing that "those scroundrels . . . should come round by water and bombard the village from the sea with their revolvers and Winchesters."

The details of this death scene need stressing, if only to allow us to penetrate Heyst's deepest feelings. He finally admits to Lena, with a "murmur of unconcealed despair," that she is the only one in the world who could have done what she did for him. At the very threshold of death, as Heyst slips his arm under her neck, she feels profound relief and is happy to surrender her final moments of life to him. She expires, with "a smile of innocent, girlish happiness," and with "a divine radiance on her lips," exactly at the moment when Heyst, at last, "was ready to lift her up in his firm arms and take her into the sanctuary of his innermost heart—for ever!"

In the very last chapter of *Victory*, and again from Captain Davidson's testimony, we hear of Heyst's fate. His inadequacy in the tragic events that transpired on Samburan is clearly painful to him as he surveys what has happened on an island that had originally become for him a fortress against a world he associated with betrayal and catastrophism. Heyst's despair is one that must be seen in terms of loss—the loss of his sanctuary, the loss of his "cherished negations," and now the loss of Lena, whose place in his life he finally sees as being permanent. Indeed, his last words to Davidson arise out of his recognition of his losses: "woe to the man whose heart has not learned while young to hope, to love—and to put its trust in life!"

So deep and rending are his losses in their moral import that Heyst chooses to die in the conflagration that destroys the principal bungalow, and also the other bungalows. As Davidson informs the "attentive Excellency," Heyst is ashes—"he and the girl together. I suppose he couldn't stand his thoughts before her dead body—and fire purifies everything." On the other hand, Mr. Jones, Heyst's diabolical double, suffers death by drowning, when (whether by accident or by choice), while looking for the boat, he tumbled into the water: "The boat and the man were gone, and the scoundrel saw himself all alone, his game clearly up, and fairly trapped. . . . I could see him huddled up on the bottom between two piles, like a heap of bones in a blue silk bag, with only the head and the feet sticking out." *Victory* concludes, then, on a note of death and annihilation—"there are more dead in this affair . . . than have been killed in many of the battles of the last Achin war," Davidson somberly declares.

The powerful enemy alliance resorts to all kinds of tactics in order to prevail. We have in this novel, then, a total and unconditional war going on. Heyst and Lena create a fragile and tenuous alliance that must confront a savage foe. Heyst prefers to live in a state of isolation and skepticism; and Lena seeks to escape from an oppressive captivity and find a savior who is the incarnation of love. Such an alliance of innocents is utterly unprepared for a collision with demonic forces that are absolutely certain of their aims. The circumstances of their collision are totally unfavorable to Heyst and Lena, lacking as they do any battle plan or strategy, and loyal only to the shaping spirit of their personal predicaments and destinies. Of the two, Lena is the most realistic in gauging the might of the violence in pursuit of Heyst's ostensible treasure and Lena's sexuality. Neither inwardly torn nor divided, as is Heyst, she is the more active member of the alliance. Her past exposure to evil helps her to understand what is at stake, whereas Heyst only gradually and even grudgingly discerns the full dangers of the situation once Samburan is invaded.

Conrad renders moral warfare in military detail. His battle scenes contain beach landings, forays, skirmishes, reconnaissance missions, guerrilla tactics, hand-to-hand combat, even as armies in miniature plot their strategies and execute their attacks. Even a mutinous act like Ricardo's plays a role in the struggle. There is always, too, a sense of watching and waiting when things are eerily quiet on the battle front. Climatic conditions add to the suspense, as the shadows of dark clouds touch the openings of the land, darkening even more deeply the mystery of the surrounding forest, and as thunder claps erupt and flashes of lightning pierce the skies. The anxieties, forebodings, and weariness connected with the final battle, so to speak, inevitably afflict both sides. To be sure, Conrad is revered as the "worshipper, interpreter, and prose-laureate of the sea,"[6] but, in *Victory*, his treatment of terrain, its special features, configurations, and space or extent of ground, is truly astonishing, if not prophetic when one thinks of the great land battles of the European War of 1914–1918.

Conrad employs religious imagery in this novel without at the same time making a specifically theological statement, or claim. Heyst's Christlike aspects and Lena's saintly and self-sacrificing acts in behalf of the man she believes is her savior, needless to say, have their Christian prototypes. Heyst is called to give his witness, and Lena to experience martyrdom. The religious and, more specifically, Christian concepts of Good and Evil effect the novel's total economy. Heart, mind, and soul testify to the Pauline command, "Be not overcome by evil, but overcome evil by good."[7] Even Heyst's last words to Davidson echo the Evangelist's admonition, "Beloved, let us love."[8] How is one to "overcome the world"?[9] This is a religious question that this novel wrestles with ferociously. No less significant is Conrad's use of the word victory. Lena and Heyst ultimately illustrate forms of "victory which overcometh," since victory is given to "them that are worthy."[10]

That one cannot be "above the battle," as Heyst would like to be, is a very important lesson of *Victory*. The war being fought in this novel is not simply for treasure, or for supremacy and aggrandizement. In the final analysis, this is a war for the human soul, and, more specifically, for the spiritual part of human life considered in its moral aspect. Heyst clearly wants to neutralize his soul by isolating himself; he wants to protect his autonomy through inaction and withdrawal. Such a desire is the kind of illusion that Conrad exposes again and again in his fiction. Moral warfare, as he shows in *Victory*, cannot be exiled or transcended. No island can be utopia. No human being can cut off human ties. No one can escape or

---

[6]*Dictionary of National Biography, 1922–1930*, ed. J. R. H. Weaver (London, 1937) 209.

[7]Romans 12:21.

[8]First John 4:7.

[9]First John 16:33.

[10]First John 5:4; 2 Maccabees 15:21.

renounce the world, for the world will follow one wherever one goes and whatever one does. One must face the world, Conrad seems to be saying, even when one refuses to affirm it.

The last word in *Victory* is "Nothing!" But the very last word of this novel, written on May 29, 1914, as Conrad informs us in his "Note to the First Edition," was the single word of the title itself. It was also the last word he had written in peace time, before the coming of the European War. For Conrad the word "Victory" signified "the shining and tragic goal of noble effort." His definition is especially pertinent to the meaning of this novel. Throughout we can observe moral warfare that rages between those who value and those who would devalue human meaning. In the end, *Victory* is the story of the moral transformation and fate of human beings who are thrown into, even stricken in, the realm of gravity, and yet who cannot be denied the possibility of entering the realm of grace.

Chapter 4

Nostromo

I

In *Nostromo* (1904), as the literary critic F. R. Leavis observes, Joseph Conrad presents a public theme confluent with private histories, each one of which gives us a private theme. "These histories," Dr. Leavis goes on to say, "are of the main characters, each of whom enacts a particular answer to the question: What do men find to live for—what kind of motive force or radical attitude can give life meaning or direction?"[1] This is essentially a moral question that *Nostromo* seeks to scrutinize in carefully rendered detail, and ultimately to judge in discrete and proving ways. Transcendent life principles and values are in decisive evidence here and wield discriminatory power in the unfolding story of Conrad's novel.

The question posed by Leavis is, in fact, at the moral center of *Nostromo*: It is one with which the characters themselves must struggle, and in which the reader inevitably finds himself an active participant. The answer to this question requires effort, for in order to answer it the reader must plunge to the depths of one's being, there to confront the full, exposed self in all of its extremities and severity of self-appraisal. This process is a demanding one, heightened as it is by the particular configurations of the novel's locale, set in a Latin American state, in the town of Sulaco, a coasting port on the Atlantic seaboard of the republic of Costaguana, situated "in the solemn hush of the deep Golfo Plácido as if within an enormous semicircular and unroofed temple open to the ocean, with its walls of lofty mountains hung with the mourning draperies of cloud."

Early on in the novel we become aware that the visible signs of "the sanctuary of peace sheltering the calm existence of Sulaco" are cruelly deceptive. Disorder in the form of recurrent military revolutions plagues Costaguana. Social and political breakdown is clearly the "public theme" that *Nostromo* registers, and that affects the "private histories" and destinies of the novel's characters. Here we collide with the agents of

---

[1]Joseph Conrad, *Nostromo* (New York, 1960; 1904) quoted from F. R. Leavis's foreword, ix.

destruction—with "revolutionary rabble," a "crazy mob," murdering "bandits," as Conrad describes them. Confronting these insurrectionists in all their wrath is a strong theme in this novel. But the insurrectionism is intimately tied to men and women who define their internal character, or lack of character, in terms of their role and conduct in a world in constant flux.

Moral responsibility and courage of character are being constantly tested by radical conditions of change, as Conrad proceeds to portray how particular values of character come under attack. The intense political drama of the novel is a kind of stage on which Conrad's people enact their personal fate. Terror is the emotion that reveals itself and that shrouds the stage, with sheer human survival being a common instinct. What especially accentuates the drama is the conflict that touches everything and includes everyone in *Nostromo*. The conflict that rages in Sulaco is ultimately impervious to first principles and fans confusion, faithlessness, betrayal, opportunism, profiteering, savagery. Both the life of the community and the life of the soul mirror the magnitude of moral warfare.

Foreign business interests called the Oceanic Steam Navigation Company (O.S.N.) control Sulaco, known as the Occidental province. To this "way-out-of-the-way place," once historically important as the seat of the highest ecclesiastical court, business enterprise would bring "more steamers, a railway, a telegraph cable"—in short, a future worth materially far more than any ecclesiastical past, or any center for local trade in oxhides and indigo. "Civilized business," in other words, will not also be bringing to Sulaco the engineering and machinery that would help bring progress and development, thus transforming a place known for its "blind conservatism" into a modern "outpost of progress." Sir John, "the man of the railways," is working closely with the board of the O.S.N. Company "for the good of the republic." He has come from London specifically to study plans for the building of a great railway line in a provincial, mountainous area, with lurking dangers, but it is also an area that presented to the great "man of affairs" and to the engineer-in-chief surveying the railroad track an enormous challenge that "generated a power for the world's service."

Significantly the chief engineer is innately aware of limitations, and his words contain an ominous warning: "We can't move mountains!" Clearly the attainment of this formidable task would not be easy. "But the work would be done: the force would be almost as strong as faith." Some of the aristocratic old Spanish families of Sulaco, to be sure, would oppose "the undertaking," but, as we are told, the influence of the Englishman Charles Gould, the chief administrator of the San Tomé silver mine located "in the mountains three leagues from the town," was favorable to the new railway, and would be pivotal to silencing any opposition.

The history of the San Tomé silver mine reflects precisely the costs of material progress in human terms: "Worked in the early days mostly by means of lashes on the backs of slaves, its yield had been paid for in its own weight of bones." The mine itself becomes a symbol of relentless foreign exploitation and the pursuit of power and profit and influence. Even when the mine had been at one time abandoned and forgotten, the direct consequence of its imposing costs in both natural and human contexts, it still awakened new ambitions and never-ending dreams of wealth. As such the San Tomé mine has universal meaning, representing as it does an object of intense material desire, however tainted its inner value is, whatever the injustice, persecution, and outrage that the mine ordains, even condemning as it does one who owns (or works in) the mine to live in a "cavern of thieves, intriguers, and brigands."

From the opening paragraphs of *Nostromo*, Conrad evokes the danger of illusion when he describes the peninsula of Azuera and "a wild chaos of sharp rocks and stony levels cut about by vertical ravines," located on the other side of Sulaco, utterly waterless, far out at sea, and best known by the common folk of the region for its "forbidden treasure." Here, it is reputed, "impious adventurers" had, "within men's memory," disappeared in frantic search for gold. Two wandering sailors, "americanos, perhaps, but gringos of some sort for certain," still live among the rocks, "under the fatal spell of their success. Their souls cannot tear themselves away from their bodies mounting guard over the discovered treasure." This story casts a dark, intervening shadow over the events that will occur in the novel. It conveys a dire prophetic warning to the reader that this novel is one of fatality, of men and women who become victims of their grand illusions, even of their ideals and dogmas; who are incapable of surmounting their obsessions; and who, like the legendary lost sailors guarding forever the "forbidden wealth" in "the deep precipices cleaving the stony levels of Azuera," have no hope of release from "the tyranny of time."

Thus, the silver mine excites unending wonder and mystery and concern from generation to generation, as it does with the Goulds, who have been established in Costaguana for three generations and who inherited the "Concession" in the Sulaco province of the Republic. What the mine signifies and yields becomes a passionate interest, especially for Charles Gould, who by the age of twenty had fallen under its spell and eventually becomes its slave. For young Gould, the San Tomé mine eventually becomes his vision of power—power over material things; power into which to pour one's deepest passion, belief, thought, energy; power to defy all limits, human and divine. This vision reveals itself to him as the potential of "the tearing of the raw material of treasure from the earth." Adventure and conquest are, in essence, the objects of his quest. "Only in the conduct of our action can we find the sense of mastery over the Fates. For his action, the mine was obviously the only field," Conrad writes.

The San Tomé Concession, for Charles Gould, must become "a serious and moral success," once he inherits the mine following the early death of his father, who in fact wanted to get rid of the Concession and implored his son not to claim any part of his tainted inheritance in Costaguana. Charles Gould negotiates to get financial backing from "a considerable personage," Mr. Holroyd, an American financier and "the head of silver and steel interests," who had the capital resources to make the "rehabilitation" of the mine a reality—a reality that Charles's "weak" father was incapable of ever grasping.

Charles Gould is supremely "a great captain of industry" whose ambition is concretized finally in the "Consolidated San Tomé mines" with their endless resources of silver, gold, copper, lead, cobalt. To achieve his goal in the face of constant political strife and revolution requires of him steadfastness. His vision of power becomes his mistress and his destiny, as well as his exclusive moral purpose. In this respect, it can be said, he personifies the Roman virtue of disciplined dedication. In the end, the extremism of his "motive force" destroys all semblance of his love for and marriage to Emilia Gould, as he obsessively gives all his energy and time to turning the once moribund Gould Concession into "the treasure house of the world." This is by no means a small accomplishment for the direct descendant of the earlier "Costaguana Goulds," "pure-bred Englishmen, but all born in the country," who had failed in making the San Tomé mine an enduring commercial success.

The father of Charles Gould, it should be remembered, long one of the wealthiest English merchants of Costaguana, where he and his son were born, had received the perpetual concession of the derelict and forgotten San Tomé mine as a full settlement for the loss of his fortune in forced loans to successive governments. But, unlike his father, who had warned his son about "the injustice, the persecution, the outrage" surrounding any resurrection of the San Tomé mine, and who himself had been overwhelmed by the problems of the mine, young Gould had instinctively prepared himself for taking command. "Mines had acquired for him a dramatic interest." Thus, he had become a mining engineer following his studies in Belgium and France, and his investigative visits to mines in Germany, Spain, England, and Italy, where he was also to meet and court his future wife.

For Charles Gould the mine becomes not simply a business "enterprise" that provides financial reward, but one that fulfills a deeper "faith" or life-purpose. For Mr. Holroyd, with his "quiet burliness," his "insatiable imagination for conquest," with "the profile of a Caesar's head on an old Roman coin"—an imperator of business interests—Gould's "earnestness" and "determination" are advantageous to his own ambitions on both a national and an international scale. His remarks to Gould echo those of a Grand Inquisitor right out of Dostoevsky: "We shall be giving the word for everything: industry, trade, law, journalism, art, politics, and religion, from Cape Horn clear over to Smith's Sound, and beyond, too, if anything worth taking hold of turns up at the North Pole." Gould intuits Holroyd's purpose, but also distinguishes it from his own monomania. Though he finds Holroyd's intentions "distasteful" and "disagreeable"—Holroyd is "nourished in facts," whereas Gould's central aim revolves imaginatively around "the one great fact of the silver mine"—he also finds in Holroyd a man who can help him achieve his "cherished hope." "Nobody else's vast conceptions of destiny could diminish the aspect of his desire for the redemption of the San Tomé mine."

Clearly each man is using the other for his own selfish purposes; theirs is an alliance that lacks any genuine moral basis. For each, moral value is either totally relative, or totally absent, or irrelevant and obscene. *Nostromo* renders this moral paradox in all of its consequences. The novel as a whole aids a reader in measuring these consequences and in recognizing their symptoms. Conrad's aim is, hence, both subtle and clearcut; and the sixth chapter in the first part of the novel, entitled "The Silver of the Mine," in which the novel's central problem and deliberations are delineated, is significantly one of the longest in the novel. It prepares the reader for what transpires in Sulaco, especially after Holroyd promises to support Gould in the mining enterprise since he views the "pure-bred Englishman" as capable of succeeding with "the San Tomé business," which would in the end be favorable to "the Holroyd connection." (Their mercenary arrangement underscores the aptness of Ezra Pound's belief that, "Until you know who has lent what to whom, you know nothing whatever of politics . . . or history.")

For Emilia Gould, Holroyd's motives smack of "awful materialism." Her husband, on the other hand, envisions the mine as a "little rift in the darkness" of "poor Costaguana." He pins his hopes, then, on "the material interests" having the ability and the resources to bring "law, good faith, order, security" to "an oppressed people" and to a corrupt country "waiting for the future in a pathetic immobility of patience." For all of those involved, then, in the rebirth of the San Tomé mine, "[t]here was no going back" to those earlier times when Sulaco, because of its location, "had found an inviolable sanctuary from the temptations of a trading world. . . ."

As the story of the mine unfolds, we become aware of corrupt political leaders on the take and of a fraudulent political process that Gould—the "king of Sulaco"—learns to deal with for the sake of his project on the mountain. For him the success of the Gould Concession signified total war, and he would use any "weapons as could be found at once in the mire of corruption." Slowly the project expands as more people go to the mine for work, with the lights on the mountain visibilizing a new economic order of opportunity and progress. Conrad paints the entire scene with large, emphatic brush strokes that capture the dynamics of a great mining operation. "The great clattering, shuffling noise, gathering speed and weight, would be caught up by the walls of the gorge, and sent upon the plain in a growl of thunder."

Now, too, we hear the whirl of the machine and see the frenzy of activity, as an entire mountain is transformed through "the clearing of the wilderness, the making of the road, the cuttting of new paths up the cliff face of San Tomé." The waterfall no longer exists here, the fernery has dried up, and the high ravine is now "a big trench half filled up with refuse of excavations and tailings." This once resplendent, primeval scene is now obliterated, its innocence preserved only in Mrs. Gould's water-color sketch solitarily hanging on the wall of the stately Casa Gould.

Growing and prospering at an inexorable pace, the mine becomes "a rallying point for everything in the province that needed order and stability to live." There is no lack of loyal followers who enable Gould to achieve his goal and to insure the day-to-day running of the mining community. The "officials of the Concession" provide him with special talents that are required for the mine's proper functioning and for the governance of the many hundreds of native workers living in the three mining villages making up the Gould Concession. There is the governor of the mine, the old professional soldier, Don Pepe, with his "pendant moustaches, a nut-brown lean face, and a clean run of a cast-iron jaw." Then there is "Doctor

Monygham, the medical pastor," "with his twisted shoulders, drooping head, sardonic mouth, and sidelong bitter glance." And there is, not least, Father Ramon, "dried up, small, alert, wrinkled, with big round eyes, a sharp chin, and a great snuff-taker." These are subordinates who serve the mechanical principle of organization as the instruments of Gould's ambition to subjugate Matter to his own ends and, with him, "to translate the Godhead into pure mechanism," to recall D. H. Lawrence's words. And indeed they help Gould to succeed in his mission, as consignments of silver begin their routine journeys on the National Central Railway to the O.S.N. Company's building by the harbor in Sulaco for final shipment by mailboat to Holroyd's headquarters in San Francisco.

As the mine begins to exert an occult influence, it also seems to become the object of reverent worship that answers prayers for happiness and prosperity in this world, veritably a terrestrial paradise. Indeed, the mine is the defining center and the most looming presence in the novel. Around the mine gather desperate and grasping forces—financiers, politicians, engineers, opportunists, and revolutionaries, the poor and the powerful, innocents and devils. The mine, and the riches it produces and generates, creates a celebratory unity of faith anchored in the confidence of purpose, in a shared conviction that change and advancement are the new deities of salvation. It is what gives meaning to human lives and represents the surrogate god they revere, even as it also represents "the very paradise of snakes"—"without rectitude, without the continuity and the force that can be found only in a moral principle."

In time the Gould Concession, *imperium in imperio*, obliterates individuality and diminishes any distinguishing and refining moral value; the human community and the human soul are deprived of intrinsic value by "the dialectic of material interests." The worst and the best of the men and women who gather in Sulaco have, it seems, no indwelling or identifying virtue, once the mine grabs control of their imaginations and aspirations. Such is the dominion of "[m]aterial changes swept along in the train of material interests." Readers may sooner or later forget the names and faces of Conrad's people in *Nostromo*, but they will not easily forget how the silver mine alters human destiny and transvalues value; how it becomes an instrument of "moral degradation." "There is no credulity so eager and blind as the credulity of covetousness," Conrad writes, "which, in its universal extent, measures the moral misery and the intellectual destitution of mankind."

II

In *Nostromo*, more than in any other of his novels, Conrad is morally and judgmentally at his severest point of vision in his depiction of corruption at the heart of the human condition that leads to moral deterioration. No illusion, no false promise, no false prophecy is permitted to impede a reader's view of the process of corruption as it afflicts humankind. In particular Conrad seeks to disabuse us of our beliefs in man's natural goodness or in any romanticist, sentimental, or utopian notion of human existence. *Nostromo*, this "most anxiously meditated of the longer novels," reveals an unwavering moral absoluteness that spurs the novelist, with "as cool a hand as was possible," to portray men and women in their elemental selves, as Conrad wrote in his 1917 "Author's Note" to the novel. His words are especially pertinent to his characterization of Charles Gould as "the idealist-creator of material interests whom we must leave to his mine—from which there is no escape in this world."

War and revolution continuously shake Sulaco and highlight the permutations of "those confounded Costaguana politics" existing sometime in the middle of the nineteenth century. In the midst of social unrest and political disarray, the mine unfailingly authenticates the story of Gould's effort "to keep unchecked the flow of treasure he had started single-handed from the reopened scar in the flank of the mountain." No private history attains full explication outside of the shadow of the mine. To be sure, Conrad as novelist provides the required details that flesh out the lives of his men and women here, but in the end we also know and recall them not as distinct human personalities but as a collectivity of vulnerable human beings.

In each of Conrad's fictive characters in *Nostromo* we see an assailable human being, ultimately unable to change one's fate or that of the universe. If anything they give constant witness to the state of disequilibrium; their personal histories lack any real or distingushing sense of spiritual meaning or ascent. Confusion and, in the end, nullity are the basic qualities of an existence brutally trapped between political tyranny and material greed. Here, in fact, Conrad's "aristocracy and people, men and women, Latin and Anglo-Saxon, bandit and politician," remain largely static characters. Their immediate historical and personal situation is one in which they seem to have no organic connection and no permanent loyalty except to the immediate moment or passing event. Presentism is their place in time, and their captivity.

If the Europeans of Sulaco give the appearance of being stereotypical exiles, the native inhabitants seem to be totally faceless, mere pawns in the hands of self-serving leaders who decide all socio-political questions with reference to the silver mine. Genuine integrity, as such, is notably absent as we view a series of newly installed governments in the Occidental Province of the Republic of Costaguana in the wake of recurring revolts. The fate of silver is the paramount concern. If, too, the value of character itself has any place in this novel, it is subordinated to the dictates of silver and the hegemony of the San Tomé mine. Thus the mine represents, variously, progress, speculation, prosperity, profit, but ultimately it embodies despotism over body, mind, soul. One can neither deny nor escape its reality of power. Conrad's people, one and all, become both the slaves of illusion and the victims of an empire of might, as it were, that induces physical and spiritual death.

The world of Sulaco is a spiritual wasteland in which human growth is an impossibility, once "terrible simplifiers" spawn their life-negating agenda and schemes of social engineering that would settle, once and for all, the "economic question." Conrad's figures here live in a veritable prison house in which life-purpose has no superior force of truth or perception of transcendence, no idea of moral heroism. Positives in *Nostromo*, it seems, are always in a state of devolution, underlining, according to the critic Douglas Hewitt, "Conrad's method of not allowing us to rest for long in a stable and comfortable attitude."[2]

The only "visible sign of the stability that could be achieved on the shifting ground of revolutions" is Charles Gould. Paradoxically, his own singular idealism as it relates to the operation of the mine reveals the same menace and intolerance one finds in the revolutionary spirit of disorder. For Gould, as he insists in defending his position to his wife, "There were things to be done. We have done them; and have gone on doing them. There is no going back now. . . . we can't even afford to stand still." Emilia Gould, "the woman with the genius of sympathetic intuition," comes, in time, to watch "his abstraction in dread," discerning in his fanatical devotion to "the material interests" and, in turn, to Holroyd, a "frightful phenomenon": "a will haunted by a fixed idea. A man haunted by a fixed idea is insane."

---

[2]*Conrad: A Reassessment* (Chester Springs PA, 1969) 51.

In one way or another, then, everyone in *Nostromo* is somehow connected to the San Tomé mine, and everything revolves around the prospects of the mine. What we have in this resultant situation, in short, is a profane world in collision with and hateful of that "moral principle" belonging to the "permanent things." Strife is everywhere, and no one escapes its sting. Conrad's belief that "the life-history of the earth must in the last instance be a history of a really very relentless warfare" encapsulates the nature of the events that transpire in this novel.

The world of nature in which warfare takes place intensifies the magnitude of the strife between man and man, and between man and creation. The landscape surrounding Sulaco has a stillness and yet a harshness that is reflected in the surrounding mountain range. The assault on the senses is dramatic: A stalking bird of prey, as we find at one point, suddenly appears in the blue, stealthily and silently circling overhead, "with an air of voracious anxiety," waiting for a chance to strike, watching, lingering—"morose and reluctant . . . circling noiselessly with a sinister droop of beak and claws." At another point we glimpse a big owl, "with a soft flutter and oblique flight . . . whose appalling cry—*'Ya-acabó*! *'Ya-acabó*! (It is finished; it is finished)—announces calamity and death. . . . " And at still another point in "the profound silence," we hear "the shrilling of innumerable cicalas in the dry grass," deafening to the ears. Conrad enlists sounds and scenes of terror as a prelude to dissolution. "Death stands near behind us all," muses one of the characters.

Conrad's natural world ultimately lacks a redeeming beauty or peace or joy. It is almost a subterranean world in which one is easily lost, in which loyalties clash, in which lives are snuffed out and souls are crushed. Anathemas ring out again and again, and resound in mountains and bays, islands and ravines and jungles, day and night, in a world now deeply scarred by a railway line for the exportation of silver to hungry hands in the north. For miles and miles the area around the silver mine has been assaulted and ravaged by engineers, planners, and technicians in pursuit of treasure, at the behest of business magnates in quest of power over nature's bounty.

The rape of nature images the atrocities found in *Nostromo*. Nature here, as in Conrad's other novels, is not one of pristine beauty, but one containing potential traps, enticements, devils. One violates such a world at one's peril Conrad seems to be saying. He does not, in effect, romanticize or glorify the natural world by exaggerating either its resources or its splendors, colors, verdures, or evoking its aura. Certainly he perceives and respects nature's marvels, but at the same time he is assiduously measuring man's limits in taming and changing the natural world in terms of costs and consequences.

Political instability never ceases in *Nostromo*. All sorts of treacheries will be committed in relation to the San Tomé treasure, and loyalties will change overnight in relation to the status of the silver nuggets. No moral constancy of belief is maintained, and even its strongest defenders surrender to compromise, inaction, doubt, temptation. Accordingly, around Sulaco there are to be seen both revolutionary and counterrevolutionary forces, commanded by arrogant leaders to whom no violence is too great or too small in controlling the silver en route to Holroyd and his business associates who are the "drawers of water and hewers of wood to all the countries and nations of the earth." If there is any single moral constancy here it is one that is shaped and manipulated by the silver treasure, at the altar of which worshippers pray for reward, and will, if necessary, sacrifice their lives, their friends and allies, their spouses and children, let alone any axiomatic principles and verities.

The religion that Conrad portrays is a political, economic, and civic religion that lacks the grace of transcendence. The people who assemble here, whether foreign or native, white or dark, seem to understand only the ineradicable fact of the silver mine and its administration, with its new hierarchs, new priests, new acolytes—and its new socio-economic faith that "generated a power for the world's service—a subtle force that could set in motion mighty machines, man's muscles, and awaken also in human breasts an unbounded devotion to the task." The republic of Costaguana emblematizes the greater modern world to come, which even the big green parrot in its cage in the Casa Gould seems to await with high expectation when it screams out "*Viva Costaguana*!"

III

Nostromo also tells the story of Martin Decoud as a man of thought, "incorrigible in his scepticism," a "man with a passion, but without a mission." A native Costaguanero, though "[n]either the son of his own country nor of any other," once a Parisian dandy, a "*boulevardier*," and journalist, "the adopted child of Western Europe," he prides himself on his power of reason. He and his family have lived abroad in Paris, where he studied law, dabbled in literature, and hoped "to become a poet like that other foreigner of Spanish blood, José María Heredia." Now, at age thirty, and after an absence of eight years, he has returned to Costaguana to support the liberal cause of Don José Avellanos, an enlightened defender of bourgeois democracy—a descendant of the old Spanish Grandees, who is essentially out of touch with the socio-political realities of Costaguana and who, old and ailing, is a casualty of political sentimentalism and romanticism.

Decoud has long been deeply in love with Don José's daughter, Antonia, an intelligent young woman, born in Europe and educated in England, who, no less than her father, is committed to her illusion of freedom and democracy for Costaguana. Decoud will now join, as an executive member, Don José's patriotic small-arms committee of Sulaco so as to perpetuate the old man's "undiscouraged belief in regeneration." He agrees to assume the editorship of *Porvenir*, a newspaper that would "voice the aspirations of the province" and oppose the lies of the revolutionaries' *Negro Liberalism.* Yet it is also clear that Decoud is far more committed to his unrequited love for Antonia than he is to a Sulaco revolution for independence. He has, he confesses, "no patriotic illusions," but "only the supreme illusion of a lover."

In any case, Decoud is enlisted in the fight against General Montero, who was leading at this point a revolt against Sulaco "in the name of national honor." At the same time he is fully aware that "the whole land is like a treasure house" exploited by foreign speculators and native insurgents alike. "After one Montero there would be another," he contends, "the lawlessness of a populace of all colours and races, barbarism, irremediable tyranny." To save Sulaco from Montero's advancing "army," commanded by the general's younger brother Pedrito, "the *guerrillero*," and also from eventual anarchy, is what motivates Decoud's actions, even as he realizes above all else that he cannot save Antonia since as an enlightened patriot she will most certainly not leave in the midst of political struggle or defeat.

As the insurgent army comes closer and closer to Sulaco, the magnitude of the threat both to the great hoard of silver awaiting delivery to Holroyd and to the San Tomé mine itself intensifies. To overcome this twin threat, Decoud devises a plan to have Sulaco secede and to become an independent country. This plan mandates the need to get the silver out of the country by loading it into a company lighter and sending it across the deep Golfo Plácido for safe delivery to a northbound O.S.N. steamer. In this scheme Decoud will work alongside Nostromo, with the main purpose to save the silver "from Montero's clutches in order to be used for Montero's defeat." The lighter with its burden of silver and with the two men controlling its fate launches into the night. Silence and darkness and the black sea are the only onlookers, as a "great recrudescence of obscurity embraced the boat."

This entire episode (memorably rendered in the seventh chapter of the second part of the novel, "The Isabels") is filled with apprehension. For Nostromo, especially, there is an overriding sense of danger in the mission to catch the steamer at sea—"for us to come to the land anywhere in a hundred miles along this coast with this silver in our possession is to run the naked breast against the point of a knife." And for Decoud there is internal anguish that arises from fatigue and from fear of the outcome, not the least of which is tied to the distinct possibility of encountering the insurgent troops from Esmeralda, the next port on the coast, and the station of the main submarine cable connecting the Occidental provinces with the outer world. Commanded by the turncoat Sotillo, these troops had gone over to Montero's party and had then taken over a government transport and were now heading towards Sulaco. Understandably, both Nostromo and Decoud are desperate men at this point, especially as their heavy boat is drifting since there is not enough wind. For them it is urgent to find the Great Isabel, the largest of the three uninhabited islets opposite to the harbor of Sulaco, the entire distance between them not exceeding two miles.

The heavy darkness and the perfect quietness surrounding the boat are like unyielding oppressors, hard to distinguish or to oppose. But suddenly an amazed Nostromo whispers to Decoud that somebody else—"somebody weeping"—is somewhere in the lighter. This dramatic scene provokes shudders, foreboding, terror. Nostromo and Decoud clamber over the "precious pile [of silver] in the middle," crouching on the foreside of the mast, and grope under the halfdeck: "Right forward, in the narrowest part, their hands came upon the limbs of a man, who remained silent as death. . . . The light of the bit of candle fell upon a round, hook-nosed face with black moustaches and little side whiskers." This man is Señor Hirsch, a hide merchant from Esmeralda. We learn that Hirsch had not been able to leave Sulaco, which was then in the midst of a riot; overcome by fear Hirsch scrambled for cover, finally seeking shelter in the O.S.N. Company's offices. He eventually crawled away to the end of the wharf and then threw himself into the lighter which contained the cargo of silver that Nostromo and Decoud would take to safekeeping. This is how he came to be found out by Nostromo, who warns him to be quiet so as not to alert the captured steamer now carrying Colonel Sotillo and his troops en route to Sulaco to capture the silver presumed to be in the customhouse.

The lighter and the invisible steamer almost touch each other in the darkness of the gulf. For the lighter to be seen or heard meant, of course, that the treasure aboard would be lost forever. Both the lighter and the steamer are lost in the gulf, immured in the dark, as it were, in sight now of the Isabels, and, in turn, Sulaco, which is Sotillo's destination. The inevitable collision now takes place, with the steamer striking the lighter obliquely, even as Hirsch's piercing shriek for help assaults the night and the rain. The shock of the collision hardly affected the steamer, while the lighter was half swamped. The steamer's anchor, we learn, was low enough to hook itself into a wire shroud of the lighter's mast, giving the sensation of the lighter being dragged headlong through the darkness. Fear and despair overpower Hirsch: "The inrush of water when the lighter heeled over unsealed his lips. His shriek 'Save me!' was the first distinct warning of the collision for the people on board the steamer." Suddenly, too, the released anchor sweeps over the lighter's forecastle, as Hirsch seizes hold of it. The steamer moves on and eventually Hirsch is discovered and hauled aboard; the lighter itself yawed off wide, not sinking, heading for the Isabels. In the meanwhile, Hirsch and Sotillo and his staff wearily conclude that a craft has been run over and sunk.

As the steamer snakes its way to Sulaco, the lighter, "leaking like a sieve," has hoisted the sail, and heads to the Great Isabel. Nostromo and Decoud are clearly aware of their common danger: "There was no bond of conviction, of common idea; they were merely two adventurers pursuing each his own adventure, involved in the same imminence of deadly peril. . . . But this peril, this only incontrovertible truth in which they shared, seemed to act as an inspiration to their mental and bodily powers." The lighter finally runs ashore, and the two men discharge its treasure of oxhide boxes containing silver ingots, to be hidden in a cavity of this "crumb of land." Decoud will remain on the island as a hiding-place, since he was wanted by the revolutionaries in Sulaco. A little dinghy was to be left with him, to be used to pull out to a passing ship. Nostromo himself will go back to Sulaco; he would use the unloaded lighter, once he had bailed it out with a wooden bucket, keeping it afloat as far as the harbor. He promises to return to the ravine for Decoud in a night or two. Nostromo realizes that the lighter must be sunk at once since his reappearance in it would raise suspicions. Hence he allows the lighter to drift with her sail aback for a while, about a mile from the harbor entrance, and then he knocks out the plug. "When he had felt her settle he sprang away with a mighty splash."

IV

The third and final part of *Nostromo*, entitled "The Lighthouse," is the longest in the novel and contains almost half of the total number of pages. This part serves to clarify the difficulties caused by a broken time-sequence that covers between fifteen and twenty years. As one critic observes: "The book begins with the beginning of the end, and the end . . . is with us throughout the entire narrative."[3] In particular, what Captain Mitchell ("Fussy Joe") has to say contributes to a more inclusive understanding of the novel's structure and import. "An old and faithful servant" of the O.S.N. Company in Sulaco, and its longtime consular agent there, Captain Mitchell reports, matter-of-factly, the shifting motions of revolution and counterrevolution in an area of the world characterized by "the lawlessness of a populace of all colors and races, barbarism, irremediable tyranny." Captain Mitchell is an inherently "good man," loyal, honest, efficient, but he has "not much penetration of any kind." Simply put, he lacks imagination and insight in perfunctorily citing "historical events" in *Nostromo*. At the time, Captain Mitchell becomes a part of Conrad's strategy to prod the reader to discern tendencies that ultimately "breed monstrous crimes and monstrous illusions."

A distinctive moral minimalism characterizes human goals in *Nostromo*: plans for reform collapse, promises dissolve, reputations founder, alliances totter, loyalties fracture, love disappoints, heroism dissipates, faith retreats. "The working of the usual institutions," we read at one point, "presented itself . . . most distinctly as a series of calamities overtaking private individuals and flowing logically from each other through hate, revenge, folly, and rapacity, as though they had been part of the divine dispensation." The only thing possible is that of some huge blowup occurring at some point in time. Charles Gould has even arranged with his second-in-command, Don Pepe, "that at the approach of an armed force he would . . . destroy scientifically the whole plant, buildings, and workshops of the mine with heavy charges of dynamite; block with ruins the main tunnel, break down the pathways, blow up the dam of the water-power, shatter the famous Gould Concession into fragments, flying sky-high out of a horrified world." This "extreme resolution" provides an apt image of the vulnerability of the political situation in Sulaco when anything can

[3]Edward Crankshaw, *Joseph Conrad* (New York, 1936) 189.

happen at any time. Nothing is ever certain, nothing is safe. And everyone, finally, is "on the spot."

Preeminent among those "on the spot" is "the illustrious *capataz de cargadores*," the head of the company's Lightermen, "a fellow in a thousand," "perfectly incorruptible": Gian´ Battista Fidanza, formerly an Italian sailor from Genoa, popularly called Nostromo. We have last seen him in the harbor as he swims away from the sinking lighter and, then, after reaching shore, falling asleep in the growth of bushes on "the ruined earthwork of the fort." At the moment of his "awakening in solitude," his "return to consciousness . . . made everything that had gone before for years appear vain and foolish, like a flattering dream come suddenly to an end." He realizes that he is no longer the celebrated figure he once was, and that he is now not only a lackey of powers much greater, but also one who is destitute: "He was as if sobered after a long bout of intoxication. His fidelity has been taken advantage of. . . . He has been betrayed." He makes his way solitarily in the night towards the ruined customhouse and becomes intrigued by the sight of two lighted windows in the abandoned building, which he enters and then climbs the stairs leading to the lighted room, in which he detects "the shadow of a man cast upon one of the walls." But he decides not to go into the room, and instead he goes down the stairs again intent on bolting from the building.

At this very moment he runs into Doctor Monygham, who is shocked to see the selfsame Nostromo believed to have been lost, along with Decoud, in the gulf. This encounter has profound consequences for Nostromo. A taciturn, cynical man, with the "outward aspect of an outcast," Monygham is distrustful of human motives. He has lived in South America for more than twenty years, drifting for a considerable time in the wildest parts of the republic. His personal history has been darkened by the fact that he had fallen into disgrace and been imprisoned by "the old tyrant," Guzmán Bento, "the 'citizen-saviour' of his country." The commission charged with examining the conspirators included an army chaplain at that time and a favorite of Bento, Father Beron. This sadistic priest, we learn, is much feared by those under suspicion for his "infliction of the most exquisite torture." Monygham could never forget his suffering at the hands of Father Beron: "his subjugation had been very crushing and very complete. That is why the limp in his walk, the twist in his shoulders, the scars on his cheek were so pronounced." Nor could he forget the pain that elicited from him information that meant certain death for those whose names he divulged as traitors. For months he rotted away "in the darkness of his gravelike prison," but later was liberated when Guzmán died from a stroke of apoplexy.

Though a broken man who is never able to absolve himself of his "shame of moral disgrace," Monygham "had made himself an ideal conception of his disgrace"; in this respect, he was to adopt an unyielding and, for him, redemptive "rule of conduct": He chooses to settle his "great fund of loyalty" on Mrs. Gould. Hence, he views the San Tomé mine and Charles Gould's deification of it as a combined danger to Mrs. Gould's emotional stability and safety. He will do anything to protect her, even if this means politically supporting Charles Gould ("in this infernal scrimmage"). Monygham concludes that a brave man must be found who will make his way overland to Cayta with a message requesting the loyalist General Barrios to return to Sulaco to help fight off the insurrectionist forces. Monygham's chance meeting with Nostromo has convinced him that the "incorruptible" capataz was the one to entrust with "the arduous mission" of reaching Barrios hundreds of miles away.

Led by Monygham, Nostromo finally discovers that "the shadow" in the room upstairs is that of Hirsch, hanging on a rope. He had been tortured and then murdered by Sotillo, who had returned to Sulaco to locate the "buried" silver and, for politcal advantage, to seize the town before the Monterist forces arrived. At this point, too, Nostromo realizes that "the only man" who knows anything about the "desperate undertaking" on the gulf can report nothing to anyone. Monygham refuses to hear from Nostromo any details of what really happened on the lighter during "the worst darkness of the Golfo." He knows from his earlier experiences that he would again be vulnerable at the hands of still another inquisitor and thus pose a serious danger to Mrs. Gould. Nostromo senses that he alone knows of the whereabouts of the silver and of Martin Decoud. Both his disillusionment (a common theme in *Nostromo*) and his new awareness that the silver can easily be his, are the ingredients of his moral corruption. The treasure has thus "fastened" upon Nostromo's mind.

Nostromo's daring mission to Cayta succeeds, and with the return of General Barrios and his troops, the Monterist forces are defeated and Sulaco is saved. Monygham was also to play an important role in the victory of the counterrevolutionary forces since he had persuaded Sotillo to drag the shallow water in the harbor for the silver, thereby giving Barrios's forces time to prevail. It should be noted that in the course of returning with Barrios on the first of the transports, Nostromo had spied from the bridge the dinghy of the lighter floating empty far out in the gulf, and, after obtaining the general's permission, he leapt overboard and eventually seized hold of and then clambered over the dinghy's stern. This was "the very boat" left with Martin Decoud on the Great Isabel. Minutely examining the boat, he saw the stain of blood on the gunwale. He now steers the dinghy towards the Great Isabel where he and Decoud had more than two weeks earlier hidden the silver. He discovers that one of the several horsehide boxes of treasure had been opened and four ingots of silver had been carried off in the boat with the blood stain. Neither the ingots nor Decoud, he concluded, would ever be seen again.

Now we finally learn the story of Decoud's fate: "The brilliant Costaguanero of the boulevards had died from solitude and want of faith in himself and others." After long delays of silence and sleeplessness, he "lost all belief in the reality of his action past and to come." Conrad's picture of Decoud's collapse is harrowing in detail. A sense of nothingness seems to have devoured him, and his intelligence and passion are to be of no avail to him as he beholds "the universe as a succession of incomprehensible images." For him failure and hopelessness are the absolutes of his doom. His actions are now those of a sleepwalker as he buckles the belt with the revolver around his waist, slits open one of the boxes and takes from it four ingots, which he puts in his pockets; he gets into the dinghy and pulls away from cliff of the Great Isabel as night approaches. At daybreak his death-journey, so to speak, comes to an end when Decoud draws the revolver from its leather case, points it at his breast, and pulls the trigger: "and the lover of Antonia Avellanos rolled overboard without having heard the cord of silence snap in the solitude of the Placid Gulf, whose glittering surface remained untroubled by the fall of his body."

Just a few days later, Nostromo, about whose death Decoud himself had wondered immediately before his own demise, appears "in nearly the same pose, in the same place in which had sat that other sleepless man who had gone away for ever so quietly in a small boat, about the time of sunset." Nostromo, too, wonders about the circumstances of Decoud's death and about the ingots, as he looks down upon "the fall of loose earth, stones, and smashed bushes, concealing the hiding-place of the silver." The final words in this chapter are Nostromo's: " 'I must grow rich very slowly,' he meditated."

The bars of the San Tomé silver have their symbolic significance in these last chapters of *Nostromo*. Decoud, on the one hand, weighted by the four ingots, "disappeared without a trace, swallowed up in the immense indifference of things." Nostromo, on the other hand, will be gradually making his fortune through the years as he periodically and secretly returns on his coasting schooner to retrieve two silver ingots at a time concealed on the Great Isabel, on which a lighthouse had been erected and of which the old Genoese sailor Giorgio Viola, accompanied by his daughters Linda and Giselle, was made the keeper. The once incorruptible captain fully feels the humiliation and the suffering "from the concentration of his thought upon the treasure." He is a broken, fallen figure whose great inner resources are rotting away as the silver progressively makes him its slave. Conrad probes deeply into Nostromo's inner terrain and the conditions of his moral degradation when he writes: "A transgression, a crime, entering a man's existence, eats it up like a malignant growth, consumes it like a fever. . . . His courage, his magnificence, his leisure, his work, everything was as before, only everything was a sham." Though Nostromo curses the silver of San Tomé, he cannot renounce either its fascination or its dominion. No less than Decoud, whose "intellectual audacity" betrayed him, Nostromo also pays the price as the "victim of the disenchanted vanity which is the reward of audacious action." The stain of moral corruption assaults all aspects of his life, including "the violence of his passion."

During his periodic visits to the Great Isabel he courts "the black-eyed Linda," to whom he becomes betrothed. But there is still another moral complexity that mars Nostromo's life: He has fallen helplessly in love with Giorgio Viola's younger daughter, the beautiful and flirtatious Giselle: "She had come upon him unawares. She was a danger. A frightful danger." Their liaisons at night flourish in secrecy, and with an erotic frenzy not often found in Conrad's fiction: "He was lost to the world in their embraced stillness. . . . Masterful and tender, he was entering slowly upon the fullness of his possession." Nostromo tells her all about the riches he was amassing, and promises to take her far away (to "a white palace upon a hill above a blue sea") once he has amassed his fortune. (He does not disclose to her where the silver is located, realizing as he does the danger of such knowledge.) The "spectre of the unlawful silver" shrouds their love with an ominous sense of guilt and menace: "He had two masters now." In the meanwhile Linda begins to intuit that something is going wrong, that something is changing in Nostromo, and she is plagued by a "sense of unreality and deception."

Nostromo is not alone in his love for Giselle. There is also a certain Ramírez, trained by Nostromo and later his successor as the capataz of the Sulaco cargadores. Giorgio Viola detested "the honest, lovelorn swain," and prohibited Ramírez from visiting the island in order to protect Giselle's honor, and "the honour of his house." Though a fleeting figure in the concluding pages of the novel, Ramírez plays a role in sealing Nostromo's fate. His moral condition is now in a climactic state of degeneration, as Nostromo moves irrevocably towards his execution for his moral outrages, in short, for his moral infidelity. Nostromo here exemplifies the man of pride in sight of his fall, which even Giselle seems to detect at the end of their love-making when she asks him: "But why have you done this blind, mad, cruel, frightful thing?"

The power of moral darkness is unrelenting in the very last chapter of the novel in which we see Nostromo engaged once again in his stealthy visits to the Grand Isabel to acquire silver and to meet Giselle. Indeed, on Nostromo's fatal day of "lying and deceiving," Giorgio Viola seems even more uneasy and suspicious regarding Ramírez's designs upon "flighty" Giselle. We find him carrying his old gun, prowling all about the island, "on watch over his honour." A distraught Linda, on that same night, still hopes to regain Nostromo's love, however "incomprehensible" she finds the situation to be. While descending the spiral stairs of the lighthouse, and upon opening the door, she "heard the first shot ever fired on the Great Isabel." Before her is her father who has shot Nostromo, mistaking him for Ramírez. Running on feverishly she reaches the cottage and sees Giselle darting past her in a crazed state. Before her she sees her immobile father leaning upon his rifle. She also hears "a murmur of despair and tears gr[owing] louder to her strained hearing." Linda now detects the formless shapes of Giselle and Nostromo on the ground. He had been caught unawares by old Giorgio "while stealing across the open towards the ravine to get some more silver."

On the following day Nostromo's body is taken to a first-aid hospital near the harbor. Now very close to death, he asks to see Mrs. Gould. The death-bed scene in "the dimly lit room" is haunting in its details as she, "cloaked and monastically hooded over her evening costume . . . bent over him with an invincible and dreary sadness." We have here in essence a confession scene: "I die betrayed—betrayed by—," Nostromo gasps, and goes on to give her details about the "accursed" silver that held him prisoner and that in the end was to kill him. He wants to tell her where the silver is, but she will hear nothing of that. " 'No, capataz,' she said. 'No one misses it now. Let it be lost forever.' " The last moments of his life are excruciating: "and the capataz de cargadores died without a word or moan after an hour of immobility, broken by short shudders testifying to the most atrocious sufferings." Giorgio Viola, "the immaculate republican, the hero without a stain," had in the meantime remained at the very place where he had "fired at the thief of his honour."

A Shakespearian poetry of tragedy infuses this final scene in *Nostromo*, as Linda now leads her father back into the house: "On the threshold he stumbled heavily. . . . His excitement, his activity of the last few days, had been like the flare of a dying lamp." The focus in the text here has a valedictory ring: For though Giorgio Viola may be very deeply confused and infirm, his presence here reveals a sincerity betrayed by those who have unconditionally adopted an ersatz religion—"the religion of silver and iron." Viola's presence, mysterious and majestic in its terror, gives lonely witness to the unselfish and unblemished truth of faith that belongs to time and eternity. He asks Linda to fetch him "the book"—"the Bible given him ages ago by an Englishman in Palermo": "[H]e never detached his eyes from the book . . . till his snow-white head rested upon the open pages. A wooden clock ticked methodically on the whitewashed wall, and growing slowly cold . . . [he] lay alone, rugged, undecayed, like an old oak uprooted by a treacherous gust of wind."

From Giorgio Viola, who served mainly under Giuseppe Garibaldi (1807–1882), "fiery apostle of independence," both in South America and in Italy, the reader gains added insight into the dynamics of revolution. Conrad portrays the old Garibaldino with sympathy as a selfless "champion of oppressed humanity," a passionate enemy of both monarchy and revolutionary mobs—"Liberty and Garibaldi were his divinities." For years he had fought by the side of "the great man who had led him in a glorious struggle" for freedom, but which he had also come to see had come to naught: "the stern devotion had cast gloom upon Giorgio's old age. It cast a gloom because the cause seemed lost." Viola personifies the heroic virtues, loyalty and honor, those virtues which, during his years as the long-time expatriate hotelkeeper of the Sulaco harbor, he was to find constantly violated in Costaguana. "A close-meshed net of corruption lay upon the country." Viola's example throws contrasting light on the motives of those in *Nostromo* who are ultimately using the revolution for personal power and financial gain. But, as Conrad clearly shows, "the venerable Garibaldino" is flawed by his "austere, old-world republicanism" and the illusions it ignited and even perpetrated, "as if the world were a battlefield where men had to fight for the sake of universal love and brotherhood, instead of a more or less share of booty."

V

The human circumstances that Conrad portrays in this novel seem to be totally devoid of grace. Moments of redemption are short-lived or else are undermined by some incipient flaw. The force of gravity seems to be everywhere unassailable; the powers of moral darkness are oppressive and pernicious in their forms of insurgency, disorder, treason, destruction, mutability. Resistance to these infernal powers, even when it emerges in an Emilia Gould or a Giorgio Viola, is rarely efficacious, and ends in benign apathy and disillusionment. They, too, are "prisoner[s] in wartime" who give abject witness to "aspirations unrealizable," and no phrase in this novel better expresses either its conundrums or its irresolutions. Some of Conrad's critics and readers will no doubt be troubled by the novel's failure to provide any definiteness of hope or to chart a way out of the "pit of corruption." As one commentator wearily concludes: "*Nostromo* is an intensely pessimistic book; it is perhaps the most impressive monument to futility ever created." Words like these in effect reduce this novel, on which Conrad labored for nearly two years ("as one would cycle over a precipice along a 14-inch plank") to "a great morality play in modern costume on the theme of human limitation."[4]

Conrad described *Nostromo* as the novel that "will always remain my largest canvass." Certainly it is the most ambitious and inclusive of his novels in probing the total moral order and speaking to the total human consciousness. Here there is neither a solitary hero who embraces the main thrust of the novel, nor a particularistic dynamic that is being evoked. *Nostromo* contains a comprehensive view of human existence, and beyond that, the universal constituents and referents that distinguish the moral order. To cite *Nostromo* as Conrad's "masterwork" is in the end to see its magnitude of value on the highest plane of world literature, of mythopoeic fiction that, like Herman Melville's *Moby Dick*, or Fyodor Dostoevsky's *The Brothers Karamazov*, or, in more recent times, D. H. Lawrence's *Women in Love*, imparts a planetary vision that passes beyond the confines of time and place, of language itself, and contemplates man and history. That vision transfigures into moral contemplation of life and history, and of the quest for ultimate reality and truth. A modern novelist who attains this artistic process, as does Conrad in *Nostromo*, inevitably shares in the

---

[4]Paul Wiley, *Conrad's Measure of Man* (Madison WI, 1954) 99.

tradition of our great ancient poets who perceive what is fundamental in human beings.

In *Nostromo* Conrad conveys his perceptions not only of politics and revolution but also of the nature of civilizational order. Above all, he shows how the absolute quest for material advantage defies the law of measure and unleashes those powers of moral darkness that smother the truth of things and the hope of better things. The structure of the novel—its movement, mood, digressions, fleeting impressions—evokes constant disharmony, as we view men and women ravaged by fanatical ideas and consumed by dreams of avarice. The consequences of this pursuit Conrad portrays with metaphoric genius that objectifies the fury and violence of a people and a land in continuous upheaval; his use of images of internecine strife and madness underscores the pathology of revolution and disorder on physical and metaphysical levels. A profane spirit rules throughout. The Hebrew prophet's words, "For they have sown the wind, and they shall reap the whirlwind,"[5] point directly to the momentum of interacting historical events and human actions. Time itself is out of joint. Nothing is certain. Nothing is at peace for long.

When, in the end, the province of Sulaco successfully attains its secession, there is no assurance that civic law and order will prevail. Discontent and unrest invariably breed new trouble and turmoil. Even as Nostromo is dying, a solitary figure suddenly appears, having been fetched by a "comrade" to look in on the "mortally wounded man." "Small, frail, bloodthirsty, the hater of capitalists," he anxiously asks "Comrade Fidanza" if he has any "dispositions" to make: "Do not forget that we want money for our work. The rich must be fought with their own weapons." Nostromo, whose death is imminent, does not answer, but rolls his head slowly on the pillow and opens his eyes, "directing at the weird figure perched by his bedside a glance of enigmatic and profound inquiry." The prophetic voice of disorder that we hear, terrible and terrifying in its forthtelling, is still another dimension of Conrad's visionary novel.

Nostromo is far more than just a novel of politics. It explores, with astonishing insight and wisdom, how human beings conduct themselves as members of the community, or better, how they define and acquit themselves in a world in which paradox and antinomy collide with human efforts and motives that shape human destiny. This process in all of its

---

[5]Hosea 8:7.

complexity, at once visible and invisible, is one into which man is thrown. The picture of existence in *Nostromo* is not rooted in a divine perspective, but in moral darkness. The evil that it portrays is incontrovertible. Clearly Conrad's task as a novelist is not one that seeks "to wander wild in its own empire of chimeras," but rather to see things as they are, and thus to render "experience vivified by the imagination," to employ the words of Irving Babbitt.[6] In *Nostromo*, Conrad frees the reader from the prejudicial traps of optimism or pessimism. Here he attains his purpose by "Seeing near things with their extensions of meaning and thus of seeing far things close up"; he is, in effect, quintessentially a "realist of distances."[7]

The extreme personal and historical situations Conrad paints in *Nostromo*, with all their distortions and aberrations and abominations, once they are penetrated, reveal to the reader undeniable truths of human meaning and experience too often and expeditiously ignored, or scorned, or shunned. How does one go beyond the veil of darkness, imaged in Shakespeare's words that serve as Conrad's epigraph to *Nostromo*: "*so foul a sky clears not without a storm*"? Darkness in this novel dominates scene after scene in the sundry forms of obscurity and blindness, of the absence of the "light" of life, of the habit of concealing the true hidden nature of things that the march of events reveals unmitigably. From the first chapter, as "Sky, land, and sea disappear together out of the world when the Plácido . . . goes to sleep under its black poncho," to the last chapter, when death goes not gently into "the bluish sheen of a night without stars," it is a darkness of spirit that pervades the novel. This darkness is a moral darkness in which legionary powers snarl and prowl in endless search of "damaged souls." In this greatest of Conrad's novels, purveyors of moral darkness are battling for victory in this world, in this time . . . here . . . now, with far-reaching consequences for both human history and man's fate.

As a "blind darkness" possesses the deep Golfo Plácido at the end of the novel, the scenario before us seems to translate into an icon on which Conrad's figures are starkly painted in muted colors and grotesque shapes, and which exudes a mood and an atmosphere at once solemn, mysterious,

---

[6]Quoted in George A. Panichas, *The Critical Legacy of Irving Babbitt* (Wilmington DE, 1999) 35, 36.

[7]The words quoted in this sentence are Flannery O'Connor's and are found in *The Added Dimension: The Art and Mind of Flannery O'Connor*, ed. Melvin J. Friedman and Lewis A. Lawson (New York, 1966) 237.

mournful: "Nostromo lying on the ground with his head in the younger girl's lap, and father Viola standing some distance off leaning on his gun"; "Mrs. Gould's face, very white within the shadow of the hood, bent over him with an invincible and dreary sadness"; "Giselle Viola, kneeling at the end of the bed, her gold hair with coppery gleams loose and scattered over the capataz's feet." And who, indeed, can forget the haunting presence of Linda, her black figure "upright on the light of the lantern with her arms raised above her head as though she were going to throw herself over"? Linda's voice is the last one we hear in the novel, and in that voice we hear a "cry of undying passion" echoing from "Punta Mala to Azuera and away to the bright line of the horizon." It is as if Conrad's icon itself now vibrates unspeakably as Linda affirms her unbounded love for Nostromo. "I cannot understand," she whispers. "But I shall never forget thee. Never!" And then her whisper magnifies into "one great cry": "Never! Gian' Battista!"

Chapter 5

Under Western Eyes

I

Valuable commentaries have been written about the sociopolitical and historical facets of Joseph Conrad's *Under Western Eyes* (1911), and of its prophetic and tragedic truths regarding pre-1917 Russia. However, the moral internals of this novel have yet to be adequately explored. Merely to mention the "moral isolation" or the "moral anarchism" that *Under Western Eyes* registers in relation to human life and destiny hardly goes far enough. Conrad invites his readers to go to the heart of the novel's happenings; that they grapple strenuously with its moral problems and experience its moral vision in both its descending and its ascending movements.

Conrad confessed in his "Author's Note," added in 1926, that *Under Western Eyes* was a failure with the reading public. Such failure is not unusual when one considers the moral demands this novel makes on a reader. Indeed, even when one considers the scenes of the novel's story, which occur in the late nineteenth century, covering a period of two years, and which are located in Russia and in Switzerland, specifically St. Petersburg and Geneva, there is really no vivid atmosphere or dramatic terrain as found in *The Secret Agent* (1907). Place has a secondary role here; and evoking spectacle is not Conrad's main preoccupation. The two cities where the actions unfold are not memorably defined and are even somewhat blurred in their distinctions. Clearly Conrad has another, metaphysical intention foremost in mind: to use ideas that the novel poses as a journey of moral discovery.

Under Western Eyes expands Conrad's view of autocracy and revolution and, more specifically, his examination of the theme of betrayal encountered in *The Secret Agent*. The moral contexts of this novel are even more heightened; and the moral probity is even more subtle, as Conrad burrows into the state of isolation, and the depth of suffering and pain of conscience that his protagonist experiences. *Under Western Eyes* was to emerge from a short story, "Razumov," Conrad was originally writing, and about which he was to remark to his friend John Galsworthy, in a letter dated January 6, 1908:

> I think that I am trying to capture the very soul of things Russian—*Cosas de Russia*. It is not an easy work but it may be rather good when it's done. . . .
>
> Listen to the theme. The Student Razumov (a natural son of Prince K.) gives up secretly to the police his fellow student, Haldin, who seeks refuge in his rooms after committing a political crime (supposed to be the murder of dePleve). First movement in St. Petersburg. (Haldin is hanged, of course.)
>
> 2nd [movement] in Genève. The Student Razumov meeting abroad the mother and sister of Haldin falls in love with that last, marries her, and, after a time, confesses to her the part he played in the arrest of her brother.
>
> The psychological developments leading to Razumov's betrayal of Haldin, to the confession of the fact to his wife and to the death of these people (brought about mainly by the resemblance of their child to the late Haldin), form the real subject of the story.

The preceding synopsis describes what essentially transpires in *Under Western Eyes*, though neither marriage nor the conception of a child takes place. The final paragraph of the letter quoted reveals Conrad's twin purpose in this novel: to examine the psychology of betrayal in relation to the inner lives of those affected by Razumov's actions and to gauge the effects of these actions in relation to the condition of Razumov's soul. It is the internalizing process of betrayal and breakdown that we view in the novel.

Betrayal ignites a cruel process of inner turmoil, moral confusion, and death. Once the conscious decision to betray takes place, all action in the novel is subordinated to the main condition that is presented: the punishing power of conscience and its effects on its victim. Conrad's explorations, moving from outer to inner levels of experience, are ultimately metaphysical in character. Always in command of the vision he is rendering, and of the moral constituents of that vision, he uses the dramatic energies of the novel to venture into the deeper psychic essences seething and surging behind and beneath and within the political tableaux of what Conrad himself calls a historical novel. Though *Under Western Eyes* recreates historical events, in space and in time, it is a novel that includes and transcends place and history in moral implications and meaning. The historical events constitute a horizontal line of action with specific reference points of place and time and race. In his note Conrad provides some hint of the vertical significance of his novel, of what later in the text itself he speaks of as the task of the novelist to eventuate "the moral discovery which should be the object of every tale." In this note, Conrad stresses the fact that the historical actualities that he is rendering in the end translate into the conditions and circumstances that subsume human existence and that demand a transcendental understanding.

> The ferocity and imbecility of an autocratic rule rejecting all legality and in fact basing itself upon complete moral anarchism provokes the no less imbecile and atrocious answer of a purely Utopian revolutionism encompassing destruction by the first means to hand, in the strange conviction that a fundamental change of hearts must follow the downfall of any given human institution. These people are unable to see that all they can effect is merely a change of names.

The political events of the novel, chiefly the assassination in St. Petersburg of a prominent and powerful Russian statesman, give the novel political specificity, that is, pre-1917 Russian autocracy. This assassination is depicted in the light of a social-political milieu of tyranny, terror, oppression, corruption. The Tsarist government is relentless in its efforts to maintain absolute rule in the face of sporadic outbreaks of revolt and disorder. We encounter a totalitarian state that brooks no challenge to "the principle of autocracy"; and no one who comes under the slightest suspicion of disloyalty, even of dissent, escapes watching. The murdered government official, the Minister-President Mr. de P—, epitomizes the totalitarian mentality in its obsessive fear of sedition, as well as its fanaticism in keeping the status quo—"he was bent on extirpating from the land every vestige of anything that resembled freedom in public institutions; and in his ruthless prosecution of the rising generation he seemed to aim at the destruction of the very hope of liberty itself."

His assassin, Victor Victorovitch Haldin, a student at the University, takes refuge in Razumov's lodgings following the murder, remaining there for several hours before the latter's arrival. The two young students were never on intimate terms, nor were they "in exactly the same camp," though Haldin knew of and admired Razumov for his solidity of character "which cannot exist without courage." Almost immediately he tells Razumov that it was he, Haldin, who had "removed" Mr. de P—, "a dangerous man—a convinced man." He goes on to relate the details of the murder plans and of the murder itself. He also notes that, after the assassination, he walked quickly to one of the poorer sections of the town in order to find Ziemianitch, a town-peasant and owner of a small number of sledges and horses for hire, who had once indicated his willingness to lead the assassin to safety. Haldin, failing to find Ziemianitch at his usual haunt, a low-class eating house on the outskirts of town, at first hid in a nearby woodyard, but from which he was ejected by the watchman. He then repaired to Razumov's rooms, keeping in mind not only Razumov's reputation, but also the fact that the latter was "the last person that could be suspected" by the authorities. From Razumov he seeks help "to vanish," and asks Razumov to find Ziemianitch and to make a final arrangement for his getaway.

Razumov's response to this dangerous situation, with all of its perils, is one of "anger," "hate," "indignation," "dismay." Basically, too, Razumov is detached and apolitical in his views. A student of philosophy at the University, he sought for academic recognition, and, hence, he was concerned chiefly with his own work, his studies, and his future. This sudden contact with an assassin and traitor now endangered Razumov's modest and normative goals. He saw himself implicated in a political crime with which he had no connection and no special sympathy, and he intuited the dire consequences: "Razumov saw himself shut up in a fortress, worried, badgered, perhaps ill-used. He saw himself deported by an administrative order, his life broken, ruined, and robbed of order." For him Haldin represents the enemy who has now violated his raison d'être and who embodies the threat of breakdown. In a sense Haldin is the destroyer of Razumov's ordered, if not innocent, world. Extremism, in a word, now invades Razumov's private world; and he feels overpowered by its antagonist spirit; indeed, this can even be termed the spectre of ideology casting a dark shadow over human existence.

Haldin himself manifests the kind of threat, and even evil, that frequents Conrad's fictional world as a whole—"I am the world itself, come to pay you a visit. . . . I am a sort of fate—the retribution that waits its time," to recall the words of that "envoy of the outer world," Jones, in *Victory* (1914). And Razumov is still another "unarmed man" encountering yet another "envoy of the outer world" who fills him with fear, about which Conrad writes in "An Outpost of Progress" (1898): "A man may destroy everything within himself . . . but . . . he cannot destroy fear." Indeed, from the moment of his encounter with Haldin it is fear that possesses and drives Razumov in all of his actions—his moods, feelings, and decisions that would permanently, even fatally, affect him and also the lives of those who come into any contact with him.

Increasingly the external world presses against Razumov's world of solitude and the sense of order that it seems to provide him. His isolation defines and strengthens his control over his life. In recognizing the limits of his rarefied situation, he achieves the virtue of measure enabling him to deal with his situation. Thus, in his contacts with his contemporaries he maintains detachment, even as he is always a good listener who scrupulously kept a certain dispassionateness along with intelligent understanding and even friendliness. But he is also one who has formed no binding ties or commitments that would distract him from his defined goals. Within his limit-situation he steered with care, as Conrad would put it. His was a life of regularity, of openness, of steadiness, which the authorities, no less than his peers, esteemed for its future possibilities.

In his "Author's Note," Conrad speaks of Razumov with sympathy: "He is an ordinary young man, with a healthy capacity for work and sane ambitions." But, as Conrad also goes on to declare, Razumov is, like many Russians, both the oppressors and the oppressed, a victim "of the normality of their place, and time, and race." "The sanguinary futility of the crimes and the sacrifices seething in that amorphous mass envelops and crushes him." As Conrad also emphasizes, this process of destruction is fueled by that most curious of alliances, autocracy and revolutionism, and the terrors which that alliance unleashes. The chord of sympathy which one hears in this novel, and which gives it its quality of feeling, is one which emerges from what Conrad descried as the social-political nullity that he probes in these revealing sentences of his note, which crystallize Conrad's prophetic estimation of the pitfalls of a warped ideology that demean the human spirit:

> The ferocity and imbecility of an autocratic rule rejecting all legality and in fact basing itself upon complete moral anarchism provokes the no less imbecile and atrocious answer of a purely Utopian revolutionism encompassing destruction by the first means to hand, in the strange conviction that a fundamental change of hearts must follow the downfall of any given human institutions.

From the beginning to the end of the novel, Kirylo Sidorovitch Razumov mirrors the state of isolation and its inescapable affliction. His parentage was not clearly known, and it was said that he was the illegitimate son of a distinguished nobleman, Prince K—, who was also his protector. His deep sense of being alone in the world, fated to fend for himself, to endure and, if possible, to succeed in the world, at all costs, makes him all the more apprehensive. He realized that to be implicated in any revolutionary activity "meant simply sinking into the lowest social depths amongst the hopeless and the destitute—the night birds of the city." These thoughts attack the very center of Razumov's being, reinforcing his sense of isolation and defenselessness.

The presence of Haldin locked up in his rooms drives him into fury, and he is obsessed with "the desperate desire to get rid of his presence which drove him forward." When he finds that Ziemianitch was not at the low eating house, he is dumbfounded. The owner of the den volunteers to take Razumov to a nearby building—"through a small doorway into a long cavernous place like a neglected subterranean byre." And here he discovers the prone body of Ziemianitch, in a drunken stupor, unable to be awakened even when kicked by the eating-house keeper. The sight of "the man of horses," who alone could save Haldin and in turn Razumov himself, is alarming: "A terrible fury—the blind rage of self-preservation—possessed Razumov." He is so infuriated that he seizes the handle of a stablefork and strikes the prostrate body before him: "Razumov belaboured Ziemianitch with insatiable fury, in great volleys of sounding thwacks."

For Razumov, both Ziemianitch and Haldin signify entrapment. "Between the two he was done for. Between the drunkenness of the peasant incapable of action and the dream-intoxication of the idealist incapable of perceiving the reason of things, and the true character of men." His thoughts return incessantly to Haldin, "the guest he had in his rooms," and whom he likens to "a pestilential disease that would not perhaps take your life, but would take from you all that made life worth living. . . . " He even considers killing Haldin when he gets home, but he knew that such action would solve nothing. Infinitely shaken, he sees himself as a condemned man with "no exit": "He had not even a moral refuge—the refuge of confidence."

Clearly Razumov is an honorable man now face-to-face with a dishonorable world. A man of reason, as his name signifies, he comes more and more to reject everything Haldin represents. "Haldin means disruption," he tells himself, as he walks slowly on "the soft carpet of snow" of "his native soil," and as he envisions "a passive land with its lives of countless people like Ziemianitch and its handful of agitators like this Haldin—murdering foolishly." "If I must suffer," he tells himself, "let me at least suffer for my convictions, not for a crime my reason—my cool superior reason—rejects." Conrad renders this scene in which Razumov holds a discourse with himself, step by step, and with dramatic intensity. Razumov is obsessed with Haldin, what he is, what he has done, what he portends. And though he does not want his death, he sees Haldin as one who cannot possibly be saved. It is too late. Here his rational faculty speaks to Razumov directly, unsentimentally, and without illusions: "If I must perish through him, let me at least not perish with him, and associated against my will with his sombre folly that understands nothing either of men or things."

During this entire episode Razumov appears as a man in deep moral concentration, fully aware of the severe consequences of his decision: "*I shall give him up*." That this decision denotes an act of betrayal does not trouble Razumov since he also believes "that there must be a moral bond first. All a man can betray is his conscience." And now, following agonizing personal discourse, he gets into a sledge and orders the driver to take him to Prince K—, who receives him in his study; after the passage of a half hour, they are both on their way to the house of General T—, to whom Razumov, with loathing, utters the name: "Victor Victorovitch Haldin." Razumov then returns to his rooms. The scene here is dark and eerie as Razumov lights a match to find Haldin still lying flat on his back in the bed. "Razumov thought suddenly, 'I have walked over his chest.' " And to Haldin he says, in a muffled voice, "It's done." That is, to say, he has made arrangements with the authorities for Haldin's escape. The betrayal scene is bathed in somber colors, with intermittent ironies of silence, echoing doom, when, at three minutes to the midnight hour, one condemned man chooses to condemn another man to death. Haldin departs, quietly and portentously: "There was a faint rustling in the outer room, the feeble click of a bolt drawn back lightly. He was gone—almost as noiseless as a vision."

The act of betrayal has a rending inner effect as feelings of agitation besiege Razumov and heighten the torments of his isolation: "Several times that night he woke up shivering from a dream of walking through drifts of snow in Russia where he was completely alone. . . . " On the day following his act of betrayal Razumov learns from another student of Haldin's arrest. And an official letter he receives commands him to present himself promptly at the General Secretariat, where he is to meet with Gregory Matvieitch Mikulin,—chief of a department who happens to have a more humane aspect, as indicated when he first receives Razumov: "The mild gaze rested on him . . . almost without passion. In its passionless persistence there was something resembling sympathy." Razumov learns directly from Councillor Mikulin that Haldin was hanged at four o'clock that same afternoon.

The meeting of the two men is painted in a calm, almost detached manner, the entire scene evoked with a sense of fatality: "The silence and immobility of Councillor Mikulin impressed him [Razumov]. The bearded bureaucrat sat at his post, mysteriously self-possessed like an idol with dim, unreadable eyes." Mikulin, and, no doubt, the authorities rightly perceive the magnitude of Razumov's plight: they know that he has nowhere to go, that, in fact, his fate, too, is sealed. They know that they have him in their pocket, so to speak. Mikulin is simply allowing Razumov to speak his thoughts without restraint or any threat of punishment, knowing that Razumov's betrayal of Haldin makes him a marked man for the rest of his life. When Razumov cries out that he has "the right to be done with that man, Haldin," that he can resolve everything by choosing "To retire—simply to retire," the "seated bureaucrat" calmly and softly asks, "Where to?" Part First ends with these ominous words.

By now, too, we are made aware of Razumov's moral predicament, no less than his moral isolation, condemned as he is by both "the lawlessness of autocracy" and "the lawlessness of revolution." What is made unmistakably clear by the end of this first movement of the novel is that Razumov's private world is now in shambles. Haldin, as Razumov declares to Mikulin, exemplifies "Visionaries [who] work everlasting evil on earth. Their Utopias inspire in the mass of mediocre minds a disgust of reality and a contempt for the secular logic of human development."

And the beneficent world, too, that Razumov envisioned, we are reminded, is unattainable. This beneficent world he was to summarize in a piece of paper on which he wrote five lines, one under the other:

> History not Theory.
> Patriotism not Internationalism.
> Evolution not Revolution.
> Direction not Destruction.
> Unity not Disruption.

Razumov wrote these words ("a sort of political confession of faith") following Haldin's departure from his lodgings; and he was to stab the paper with a penknife to the wall at the head of the bed. The police found this paper when they searched Razumov's rooms.

II

Haldin's mother and sister, Nathalie, lived in Geneva, where they eventually expected Haldin to join them, and then go to Italy together. It is here that the Haldin women, as Russian émigrés, learn of his capture, judgment, and execution. Conrad's portrayal of their grief is unalleviating. The fate of Haldin has powerful consequences, as Nathalie indicates: "What have we to look for in the future? For what hope and what consolation?" In this novel, as in his others, Conrad once again underlines an existential concern with the future—"an idea without a future," "waiting without faith," "waiting without hope" as he has variously written elsewhere. And in this novel, too, he counts up for the reader what Robert Penn Warren speaks of as "the cost of awareness." And the costs, for the mother and her daughter, as for Razumov, are severe. Mrs. Haldin slowly wastes away, unable to cope with the death of her son. "Death," Conrad, writes, "is a remorseless spoliator." The aged mother is simply unable to accept the report of Victor's death—"to abandon him quietly to the dumb unknown."

The novel's narrator, an Englishman and a teacher of foreign languages who lives in Geneva, expresses Conrad's own feelings about revolution and about political upheaval in general. Far from being a "reactionary," Conrad's assessment of the makers and results of revolution is a caustic one of political reality and adroitness. In a "real revolution," he emphasizes, which is "not a simple dynastic change or a mere reform of institutions," the best people do not always come to the front. To be sure, the more noble human natures may begin a revolutionary movement, which then too often passes away from them and falls into the hands of fanatics and shams. Noble natures are not, Conrad declares, "the leaders of a revolution. They are its victims: the victims of disgust, of disenchantment—often of remorse. Hopes grotesquely betrayed, ideals caricatured—that is the definition of revolution."

Geneva is now the scene of Razumov's activities as a secret agent for the Russian government. Betrayal is Razumov's albatross, it is what attacks and possesses his conscience, and what shapes and seals his fate. In contact with Razumov, the reader, no less than the Haldins, the omniscient narrator, and the Russian revolutionaries themselves, is in contact with the metaphysical dimension of betrayal, which brings to mind Gabriel Marcel's observation that "we live in a world where betrayal is possible at every moment, and in every form: betrayal of all by all and of each by himself." For Razumov the act of betrayal is also his tragedy. The novel recreates the stringent moral ramifications of Razumov's tragedy, which actually goes beyond the political and ideological elements. It is the moral life that is on trial here. Razumov's thoughts and activities are detailed through the narrator's use of Razumov's journal, or diary, containing dated entries in a narrative form, covering months of time and extending over dozens of pages. The reader in effect takes part in Razumov's intense experience with empathy and even with growing, if also fitful, moral discernment, which is Conrad's overarching concern in this novel. The political and historical specificities, including Conrad's own detestation of things Russian, are in the end absorbed and transfigured by Conrad's commitment to establishing the "moral complexion," the "moral character" of the novel.

It is Conrad's principal aim in this novel to register suffering and guilt in relation to moral crime, as well as to present, in profoundly dramatic terms, the moral aspect of the confusion that conduces disorder, in both the outer world and the individual soul. The uneven structure of the novel that perturbs some readers and critics actually augments the moral confusion the novel seeks to dramatize. To be able to fathom the insidious forms of moral confusion, and all their consequences, constitutes still another major task of the novelist here. The difficulties of attaining this discernment, the obstacles and the impediments thrown in the way of discernment, are important, if not intrinsic, parts of the novel's structure. As Conrad himself was to note: "even the most artful of writers will give himself (and his morality) away in about every third sentence."

In Geneva we meet Russian revolutionists, whom Conrad portrays with astute insight and with unusual objectivity. Their illusions, romanticisms, sentimentalities, treacheries, shallowness, paradoxes are all on display here. Through them, in fact, we concentrate, sometimes exclusively, on Razumov, and penetrate his inner world. They act almost as a prism. If in *The Secret Agent* topography is employed to buttress character and to dramatize emotions and attitudes of mind, in *Under Western Eyes* a variety of men and women contribute to the delineation of Razumov's personality and problem. Place here is not pivotal in the total economy of the novel; it does not, for the most part, vivify or individuate human behavior and interrelationship. The Canton of Geneva hardly attains the tensive power of the London of *The Secret Agent*. Its bourgeois drabness excites neither Conrad nor his readers, and his reproduction of this Swiss city is routine and even somber in its details. The narration and dialogue, including internal dialogue, as well as encounters, are what ultimately develop and specify the novel's story line, and it is these elements that illuminate what happens to Razumov.

Both Razumov's moral crime and his moral isolation are amplified in his feeling "of immense moral and mental remoteness." His "bitterness of solitude" is so deep, so absorbing, that there is very little else in the outer world that can make an impression on him or cast some light on his suffering. He hears voices, sounds, but he does not really see things in their clarity. Sleeplessness and silences occupy his nights and days. He seems totally oblivious of the color and vividness of existence, as he sinks deeper and deeper into the prison of his conscience, his anguish.

At the end of part second of the novel, in the course of Razumov's chance encounter with the narrator, in the public promenade of the Bastions, they are nearing a bridge in Geneva. The Englishman appeals to Razumov to find time to visit Mrs. Haldin and Nathalie. But Razumov remains silent and removed. "He turned away . . . and leaned over the parapet of the bridge. . . . He hung well over the parapet, as if captivated by the smooth rush of the blue water under the arch." The destructive force of the current of the water under the bridge fascinates Razumov: "Its slightly undulating rush seemed capable of scouring out a channel for itself through solid granite. . . . But had it flowed through Razumov's breast, it could not have washed away the accumulated bitterness the wreckage of his life had deposited there."

In Geneva, Razumov is secretly spying on the exiled Russian revolutionists for the Tsarist régime. The revolutionists themselves view him with admiration as an accomplice, or at least as a supporter, of Victor Haldin. Conrad portrays these revolutionists with critical disinterestedness, viewing some of them as sincere or, at any rate, naive, and others as fakes. The often-stated charge that *Under Western Eyes* is merely "a Russian story for Western ears," into which Conrad poured all his Polish "hatred" of Russia and the so-called "Russian soul," steadily diminishes in the reading of the novel. To charge, with one critic, that "evil is given a local habitation and a name in Russia" grossly oversimplifies *Under Western Eyes* by regionalizing its meaning, spatially and temporally. Conrad himself was aware of the charges against this novel and defended himself on a number of occasions by insisting that he was "concerned with nothing but ideas," and that his artistic purpose was "the development of a single mood."

In this novel, he maintained, "I have approached things human in a spirit of piety," and "by establishing a standard of judgment, [I have] set their [humankind's] idealism free to look for plainer ways, for higher feelings, for deeper purposes." In the end, *Under Western Eyes* supersedes the limitations imposed on it by restrictive political interpretations. St. Petersburg, epitomizing the Russian world, and Geneva, epitomizing the West, are both equally deficient in Conrad's eyes. He was profoundly attuned to ideological deformations whether in the East or in the West. Hence, one must approach this novel in more universal ways: betrayal, political autocracy, corruption, depravity are inclusive characteristics of human existence, and go beyond geography. The human paradox, no less than the political paradox, suffuse this novel, and Conrad illuminates this double paradox in moral contexts.

The final two parts of the novel disclose this inner process of self-understanding and self-cleansing. This process is also seen in terms of Razumov's contacts with the Haldin women and the revolutionaries who gather in and around the Château Borel, "this centre of revolutionary plots, of this house of folly, of blindness, of villainy and crime." In discerning the character and the condition of these men and women Razumov reaches the point of self-discernment. That is to say, he finally confronts the nature and the consequences of his act of betrayal. These various figures are—become—embodiments of his *persona*, whether it is the hypocrisy and despotism of Peter Ivanovitch (the "burly feminist," "Russian Mazzini," and "arch-priest of Revolution"), or the sincerity and dedication of Tekla ("the *dame de compagnie*"), or the honest fanaticism of Sophia Antonovna. The process of his self-revelation emerges through his encounters with the revolutionists. He voluntarily confesses his crime, in the end, not only to Nathalie Haldin but also to the revolutionists, knowing as he does that "I am a match for them all." That is to say, he knows that the revolutionists trust him, value him for "uncommon strength of character." Razumov, thus, serves as an illusion for the revolutionists: in him they see the virtues of fortitude and determination that revolutionism requires if its work is to be done. If we learn here something of Razumov's mind and thought, we also learn something of the revolutionist mind in search of redeeming paradigms. The interactions between Razumov and the revolutionists help a reader to detect the human element that creates a certain solidarity.

For Razumov, Sophia Antonovna, the veteran "woman revolutionist," poses a challenge to his sense of self, and, indeed, his own self-preservation. Their chance encounter, as related in the third section of the third part of the novel, takes place at the Château Borel, by the gate. (The two had previously met in Zurich.) In her presence Razumov experiences feelings of vexation, even self-recrimination, as he responds, instinctively, to the intentness and gravity of her commitments to revolutionism. Depth of discernment clearly marks this dedicated woman, who seems to understand so much, to see sympathetically into the human psyche, and to convey such a piercing integrity, that "he judged her . . . as being a distinct danger in his path." She has power to arrest his thought, to pierce his secret self, to challenge his willpower. In short, she is able to "read" him in ways that others could not: "What's the matter with you," she tells him, "is that you don't like us." A kind of verbal duel goes on between them as they strive to assess each other, each also recognizing in the other certain powers of character, pertinacity, insight, that make them strong, friendly antagonists.

Sophia Antonovna's intuitive insights into his condition—"What are you flinging your very heart against? Or, perhaps, you are only playing a part."—unsettle him. Her specific inquiries, too, regarding some of his actions on the day of the Haldin affair further jar him. (It should be mentioned here that she is in possession of a "famous letter" from an informant containing "various minute details" regarding the fate of Haldin.) At one point, speaking of Haldin's death—"And what is death? At any rate, it is not a shameful thing like some kinds of life," she declares—her riveting words seem to stab into Razumov, who, understandably, "felt something stir in his breast, a sort of feeble and unpleasant tremor." Her words infiltrate his conscience, as he also strives to maintain his equilibrium as he fences with "the old revolutionary hand, the respected, trusted, and influential Sophia Antonovna. . . . Stripped of rhetoric, mysticism, and theories, she was the true spirit of destructive revolution. Clearly she was the personal adversary he had to meet," who even gains Razumov's admiration and respect, raising himself above the dangerous weaknesses of contempt or compassion," as he looks,

> at her white hair: and this mark of so many uneasy years seemed nothing but a testimony to the invincible vigour of revolt. It threw out into an astonishing relief the unwrinkled face, the brilliant black glance, the upright compact figure, the simple, brisk self-possession of the mature personality—as though in her revolutionary pilgrimage she had discovered the secret, not of everlasting youth, but of everlasting endurance.

In time, Razumov has the opportunity to meet other celebrated revolutionists passing through or living in Geneva: for example, the corpulent Nikita, nicknamed Necatov, who was "supposed to have killed more gendarmes and police agents than any revolutionist living," "the executioner of revolutionary verdicts"; the diminutive Julius Laspara, "this violent pamphleteer clamouring for revolutionary justice . . . confidant of conspirators, inditer of sanguinary menaces and manifestos." His meetings with the revolutionists prompt him to be cautious not "to shrink . . . [which] would be worse than moral suicide." Out of these meetings, too, emerges Razumov's decision to write down his thoughts in a notebook, which he actually begins to do in an "unfrequented tiny crumb of earth," an islet containing a couple of tall poplars and a few other trees which stood "grouped on the clean, dark gravel, and under them a few garden benches and a bronze effigy of Jean Jacques Rousseau." The narrator, it should be recalled, was eventually to get possession of the notebook and to use it in relating Razumov's life and fate.

Razumov's meetings, thoughts, writings, and conduct are invariably connected to the moral consequences of his act of betrayal. He cannot escape or hide from "the Haldin mystery"—"everywhere Haldin: a moral spectre infinitely more effective than any visible apparition of the dead." From Razumov's diary, too, we learn of the relentless rhythm of his ordeal, from the point of his betrayal of Haldin to the point of his betrayal of the revolutionists. This latter task, or mission, is entrusted to him by Councillor Mikulin: "It was to be a dangerous mission to Geneva for obtaining, at a critical moment, absolutely reliable information from a very accessible quarter of the inner revolutionary circle." Razumov's solitude of soul is also his schism of soul; both states of soul are tied to the moral anguish afflicting his whole being from the beginning of the Haldin affair. The novel tells the story of this moral anguish in all its gradations and ramifications. And from his own notebook, which he begins writing, "all alone with the bronze statue of Rousseau," we learn important details of his "mission." Self-knowledge is, of course, an important facet of his diary, as the reader enters the inner chambers of Razumov's soul—and as the drama of Razumov's life and fate—his moral complexity—unravels irrevocably.

III

Part IV of *Under Western Eyes* allows the reader both to see and to experience the full force and tension of Razumov's moral condition. Commentators who concentrate merely on the Russian side of Conrad's novel, and who respond merely to the foreignness, the grotesque incongruities and paradoxes of the Russian character and soul, as these go against Western rationality and sensibility, fail as a result to consider Conrad's transcendent concern with the moral issues, if not the moral dilemma, that this novel engages. Moral warfare, as such, attains a universal character in Conrad's work, and, in Razumov's case, this warfare has ultimate consequences. The Westerner in Conrad's narrator here, commanding as he does clarity and a rational sense, is representative of "terrible simplifiers" who define and mold "enlightened" Western society. Razumov in fact is a direct threat to a modern West that dares not grapple with perplexing moral issues or truths, as these emerge from a process of moral struggle and suffering. The cruel depth of this suffering on Razumov's part is dramatically heightened in juxtaposition to the narrator's simplistic attitudes and words, accentuating his "European remoteness."

In the last part of the novel we observe Razumov's pain of conscience, which returns him (and the reader) to Haldin's impact on Razumov's life and fate. Even at the point when the latter visits and talks to Mrs. Haldin,—"There was in the immobility of that bloodless face the dreadful aloofness of suffering without remedy,"—with the purpose of explaining her son's actions and demise (as "the moral victim of autocracy"), the memory of Haldin does not diminish one jot in Razumov's thoughts: "It's myself whom I have given up to destruction. . . . He has induced me to do it. I can't shake him off." On this same significant occasion, as he is about to leave the Haldin residence—"It was frankly a flight"—he comes upon Miss Haldin: "Her presence in the ante-room was as unforeseen as the apparition of her brother had been." His love for her, however understated and even mysterious, cannot be averted: "He had such a strong sense of Nathalie Haldin's presence that to look at her he felt would be a relief. It was she who had been haunting him now." The ante-room itself now becomes the "strange stage for an obscure drama"—the scene of Razumov's confession to Miss Haldin.

Nathalie haunts him no less than does Haldin himself. The moral pressure on him at this concluding point in the novel and in his life is unalleviating. What distinguishes him not only from the revolutionists but also from the authorities who have wedged themselves into his life is precisely his moral sense of what he is and what he has done, and where, above all, he is going. He is now confronting his moral future, and his moral *telos*, which is his unconsoling burden. That he cannot help either mother or daughter in terms of giving them some final comfort in their grievous loss of a son and a brother, that in fact his role in Haldin's life and death brings into question the very "question of fitness," are realities that he perceives as insuperable. It is clearly "too late" for Razumov to fulfill Nathalie's high expectations of him. "I have had the misfortune to be born clear-eyed," he tells her. "And if you only knew what strange things I have seen! What amazing and unexpected apparitions!"

In Nathalie's presence, Razumov has discovered that he needed her—and she was "moved by the same feeling." Here, clearly, appearance and reality collide, with irreversible consequences. The dramatic elements of this scene are heightened by words spoken by both of them: tensive and intent, punctured by lonely silences and cruel ambiguities that mark the way to confession. "You speak obscurely," she says to him. "It seems as if you were keeping back something from me." Her words no doubt pierce Razumov and point the way, inevitably, to his confession to her as the real betrayer of her brother. If, too, he has discovered his love for Nathalie, he has simultaneously discovered his conscience, which speaks to him with an honesty equivalent to that of his love. To be sure, she is unable, perhaps even unwilling, "to see the truth struggling on his lips."

Ultimately, Nathalie is the force that wrenches from Razumov the truth of his fateful involvement in Haldin's life. She insists on hearing the full "story" of his involvement, even as Razumov has been agonizing to relate it to her, fitfully, fatefully. His final words to her have far-reaching consequences:

> "There is no more to tell!" He made a movement forward, and she actually put her hand on his shoulder to push him away; but her strength failed her, and he kept his ground, though trembling in every limb. "It ends here—on this very spot." He pressed a denunciatory finger to his breast with force, and became perfectly still.

Comprehending now the full import of what has been said, Nathalie staggers and is helped to a chair by the old professor of languages, who has been an incredulous witness to the entire episode, which is rendered with intense dramatic power.

The actions and gestures that Conrad renders at this point buttress the power of the words uttered by both Nathalie and Razumov during this momentous encounter. She suddenly springs up from the chair, and then totters, to be assisted by the old professor-friend into the drawing room. A tragic pathos permeates, as the reader is witness to the consequences of Razumov's "atrocious confession":

> Away from the lamp, in the deeper dusk of the distant end [of the drawing room], the profile of Mrs. Haldin, her hands, her whole figure had the stillness of a sombre painting. Miss Haldin stopped, and pointed mournfully at the tragic immobility of her mother, who seemed to watch a beloved head lying in her lap.

The Conrad we find in these two sentences is not just an artist of genius but also an iconographer of wondrous power and insight, the added visual details of which seem to accumulate in the memorable depiction of Razumov, still present in this scene, looking on, making no sound, "standing before the empty chair." His mysterious presence is captured by Conrad's narrator in these prescient words:

> I stared at the broad line of his shoulders, his dark head, the amazing immobility of his limbs. At his feet the veil dropped by Miss Haldin looked intensely black in the white crudity of the light. He was gazing at it spell-bound. Next moment, stooping with an incredible, savage swiftness, he snatched it up and pressed it to his face with both hands.

At this point, too, Razumov departs, slamming the outer door, as Nathalie, now sitting on the sofa, presents a sad witness to the cruel events that have transpired. The old professor, in silent horror, now looks down at her: "Her hands were lying lifelessly, palms upwards, on her lap." In a languid whisper, she voices sorrow too deep for tears: "It is impossible to be more unhappy. . . . It is impossible. . . . I feel my heart becoming like ice."

What follows in the last two sections (IV and V) of part IV is an abeyant but desperate delineation of the fates of Razumov and the Haldin women. Here Geneva remains, for the most part, the locale which Conrad describes as "the serious-minded town of dreary hotels, tendering the same indifferent hospitality to tourists of all nations and to international conspirators of every shade." "Washed clean" by a heavy shower, Razumov has returned to his hotel room on the third floor, and here he commences immediately to write confessional passages in his notebook. In a "page and a half of incoherent writing" he addresses directly the reader regarding Nathalie's power over his imagination. It is through Nathalie, he writes, that Victor Haldin now haunts him; and it is she who was "appointed to undo the evil by making me betray myself back into truth and peace." And it is Nathalie to whom he first confesses his act of betrayal: "I felt that I must tell you that I had ended by loving you. And to tell you that I must first confess. Confess, go out—and perish." With the words, "No! I am independent—and therefore perdition is my lot," Razumov stopped writing.

He departs swiftly from his room and from the hotel to the street, "swept then by a fitful gust of wind," the darkness torn by a flash of lightning. He makes his way at midnight to the house of Julius Laspara where, he has heard earlier, the revolutionists are gathering, and he is invited by one of Laspara's daughters to enter, she having recognized him at once. Here still another confession takes place, to the amazement of his audience, as he commences to exonerate Ziemianitch of the arrest of Victor Haldin, and then continues with the actual details of his betrayal of Haldin to the authorities. At this point the revolutionist Nikita, "famous slayer of gendarmes," confronts Razumov in a scene awash with anger, disbelief, hostility. For Razumov this confession has freed him from falsehood and remorse, as he retreats from the room and walks to the stairs, where Nikita and three other revolutionists pin him against the wall. Nikita, with "his enormous arm," thereupon gives him a tremendous blow on the side of his head over the ear; Razumov is now completely overpowered and made helpless. Nikita delivers another blow to Razumov's other ear, after which the other assailants fling him out into the street. Nikita had purposely burst the drums of Razumov's ears, silencing him forever.

The scene is one of stark horror as we view a deafened and helpless Razumov staggering down a long and empty street. Conrad's graphic description of this scene conveys its eerie violence: "The lightning waved and darted round him its silent flames, the water of the deluge fell, ran, leaped, drove—noiseless like the drift of mist." Razumov, bedraggled, soaked, wanders off unsteadily, we are told, in the morning, after stepping right in front of a tramcar and goes under. The pitiless details of Razumov's condition mount up, as if to accentuate the costs of the pain of conscience and his confession. Physical destruction and moral forlornness seem to combine, mercilessly; his features "seemed composed in meditation." "Silent men, moving unheard, lifted him up, laid him on the sidewalk, gesticulating and grimacing round him their alarm, horror, and compassion." This tragic event, bathed in a spreading darkness of grief and suffering, returns us to Nathalie's eloquent, prayerful words spoken earlier to Razumov (in the third section)—words that, in fact, underscore Conrad's vision of the human predicament and of the human fate at the nethermost edge of grace: "Revolutionist and reactionary, victim and executioner, betrayer and betrayed, they shall all be pitied together when the light breaks on our black sky at last."

In the fifth and concluding section we learn of the fates not only of Razumov but also of the Haldin women. A muffled, pensive feeling pervades these pages of *Under Western Eyes*. Bleakness exists here, but so does compassion—and even hope. We learn of Mrs. Haldin's death, who "seemed to die from the shock of an ultimate disappointment borne in silence." Clearly Razumov, who had visited and spoken to Mrs. Haldin, had not gained her confidence: "She had not believed him"—though we are never told what exactly was said during their meeting. As for Nathalie, she now discloses a certain resignation and tranquillity and appears to the narrator, who sees her for the last time, to have transcended her hitherto "defenceless" situation. She looks forward, as she informs the old teacher of languages, to a new day when all discord is silenced; she is, according to her friend, "wedded to an invincible belief in the advent of loving concord springing like a heavenly flower from the soil of men's earth, soaked in blood, torn by struggles, watered with tears." Finally, too, we learn that Razumov was nursed by the "good Tekla," formerly the lady companion to the Egira of Peter Ivanovitch, who "had found work to do after her own heart," after she had seen a fleeing and deafened Razumov in the grounds of the Château Borel, where he had rushed for some unexplained reason, just before his crippling accident. After a slow recovery, he was discharged from the hospital, but would be a "hopeless cripple all his life," to be looked after by "Tekla the Samaritan." The information concerning both Nathalie and Razumov was completed two years after the cruel happenings, when the narrator was accidentally to meet Sophia Antonovna in Geneva; she had just returned from a secret excursion into Russia, where she had chanced to see both Miss Haldin and Razumov.

Nathalie now worked tirelessly in the center of Russia in a town, compassionately sharing her labors between overcrowded jails and bereaved homes. Razumov, Sophia Antonovna reports, lived in the south of Russia in a little wooden house of two rooms, tended faithfully by Tekla. His condition, we are told, was deteriorating, as we also learn that other revolutionists go to visit him when passing through: "He is intelligent. He has ideas. . . . He talks well, too," according to Sophia. To her, too, Razumov relates in minute details what transpired in the Laspara house. Sophia Antonovna's judgment of Razumov, as she expresses it to the teacher of languages, is not only forgiving, but also humane and wise. Her judgment undoubtedly reflects Conrad's moral sensitivity and insight; it also underlines his moral measure, which, as Conrad himself reminds us, is closely tied to the "earnest meditation" that is the ground of his imaginative vision. Sophia Antonovna's words illumine Razumov's character and fate:

> "There are evil moments in every life. A false suggestion enters one's brain and then fear is born—fear of oneself, fear for oneself. . . . but tell me, how many of them would deliver themselves up deliberately to perdition . . . rather than go on living, secretly debased in their own eyes? How many? . . . And please mark this—he was safe when he did it. It was just when he believed himself safe and more—infinitely more—when the possibility of being loved by that admirable girl first dawned upon him, that he discovered that his bitterest railings, the worst wickedness, the devil work of his hate and pride, could never cover up the ignominy of the existence before him. There's character in such a discovery."

Under Western Eyes portrays the process of moral discovery in the face of confusion, scoundrelism, anarchism. Razumov himself is finally able to distinguish the law of measure as it governs, or should govern, both human existence and individual character and fate. His confessions give us the measure of his character; they reveal a growing inner perception in sight of moral discovery. This, no doubt, is what Sophia Antonovna has in mind in her judgment of Razumov: "There's character in such a discovery," to recall here again her remark. Razumov, of course, has to pay the price for such a discovery at the hands of the vicious Nikita, who turns out to be a traitor himself, a spy—"the perfect flower of the terroristic wilderness," as Conrad writes in his "Author's Note." The people in this novel are all caught in the intricate web of the disorder of history: tyranny, intrigue, murder, revolution. "The most terrifying reflection (I am speaking now for myself)," Conrad further writes in his note, "is that all these people are not the product of the exceptional but of the general—of the normality of their place, and time, and race." Razumov is the victim of a historical process that ensnares him: "The sanguinary futility of the crimes and the sacrifices seething in that amorphous mass envelops and crushes him."

During his journey of moral discovery Razumov also finds his soul, which talks to him, prods him, heals and redeems him. If Razumov does not triumph over history, he does transcend its mundaneness after his mighty ordeal and effort. His experience, hence, is not exclusively one of salvation or of reconciliation, but instead one of self-purgation and self-discernment. For Razumov this is a penitential struggle that mobilizes an inherent capacity for moral growth and cleansing.

The Secret Agent portrays the death of the soul; it is a novel in which a rhythm of disintegration affects all levels of human meaning and action. In *Under Western Eyes* ratification of the soul is achieved by a rhythm of ascent. Conrad approached this novel with the same "scrupulous impartiality" that shaped his major fiction. His task thus entailed the added burden of vision that he explicitly identifies in this statement in his "Author's Note": "I had never been called before to a greater effort of detachment: detachment from all passions, prejudices and even from personal memories." A careful study of *Under Western Eyes* will confirm that, in this effort, Conrad obtained triumph.

Chapter 6

Chance

I

In his early, pioneering study, *Joseph Conrad* (1936), the critic Edward Crankshaw (1909–1984) was to praise *Chance* as "that rare thing, a work of fine spiritual significance and a technical *tour de force*." For Crankshaw it is a novel in which Conrad "has undertaken a spiritual revelation of extreme subtlety" and in which he discloses "the horror of spiritual annihilation." "Conrad's sense of evil has never been more intense," he further states, "than in this quiet, unmelodramatic story," which relates "a dreadful episode to the world as a whole without in the least robbing it of its own implicit horror."[1] In his valuation, Crankshaw was to confirm Conrad's own considerable confidence in *Chance* which was first published in London in 1913.

As Conrad remarks in his "Author's Note," added in 1920, *Chance* is the story of the life of Flora de Barral, a young woman who is "the helpless and condemned captive of the meanest conceivable fate." He renders her struggle in unfolding "stages" of "a life of moral anguish." As the "butt of ferocious misfortune," she becomes the victim, during a time-period of fourteen years, of unusually thorny circumstances. She is still another of Conrad's solitary figures whom the world has treated "dishonorably." In certain unmistakable ways she is a figure out of Charles Dickens, "pregnant with pathos."

Her situation can be described as being at once absurd and menacing as she repeatedly falls into unfriendly, designing hands and barely survives being totally devastated, both physically and spiritually. The cruelty of her plight testifies once again to Conrad's contention that "We live at the mercy of a malevolent world," in which the "energy of evil" surpasses the "energy of good." He renders this process with an unalleviating "vision of things." Flora is a victim not only of fate but also of rank exploitation, with her deepest feelings "trampled in the dirt out of all shape." In *Chance* Conrad thus focuses on the mysteries of the human predicament, with Flora

---

[1]Pages 132, 133.

dramatically and pitilessly illustrating "the blind working of the law that in our world of chances the luckless must be put in the wrong somehow."

Clearly, the subject of this novel is a solemn one. But as Crankshaw rightly reminds us, *Chance* is not itself a solemn novel, even if "every ounce is got out of its extremely solemn subject"; this "blessed lack of solemnity" it owes to Conrad's "exalted sense of perspective," or as the novelist himself emphasizes in the concluding sentence of his appended note, "I can not sufficiently insist upon the truth that when I sit down to write my intentions are always blameless however deplorable the ultimate effect of the act may turn out to be." In the course of our getting to know Flora, we also get to know the men and women who are part of her life and who help to explain her life in all of its paradoxes.

Chance, in this respect, provides as far as it is possible an explanation of complex human relationships, and of life in all of its tensions and changes. More than anything else this is a story that penetrates far beneath surface-meaning, that examines the inner and outer feelings, motives, and yearnings of human beings. The drama of human existence is what we view in this novel, in its men and women, in its conflicts and conundrums; the psychology of behavior, too, is a subject of increasing concern here, as Conrad burrows into the depths of human consciousness.

There is no feeling, no passion, no thought or doubt that is not explored here. Conrad leads the reader into the human depths, as were, and makes him an intimate part of the people and the events that embody the story of *Chance*. This process is not a matter of vicarious participation but one of illumination, understanding, discernment. How do we view and understand ourselves and others? This is a question the novelist is posing with a sense of urgency, of inexorability. Conrad renders the various stages of the story with steady patience and temperateness.

There is no great storm that engulfs us in *Chance*; the storm actually taking place is within the human psyche, even when it is not fully detected, or taken into account, or just gradually observed, which makes the storm eventually more fierce and frightening in scope and consequences. This storm, Conrad shows, is inescapable, containing as it does the very essence of the human predicament. The quest is not about life-answers but about the limits of life-understanding. Here Conrad is not indulging in metaphysical speculations, for he is profoundly aware of the inexplicable and the inexpressible mysteries of life that defy a finality of analysis and judgment. "There was nothing to find out, most likely," Conrad writes, querulously, for, inevitably "things are sometimes different from what they look."

Cynicism, however, is not the hallmark of Conrad's vision of things in *Chance*, for in this novel moral possibility is a theme equal to, if not stronger than, the experience of "moral loneliness," which Conrad recreates in the life of Flora de Barral. To be sure, the acute pain of suffering is pervasive in the story of Flora's encounter with the world, from the time when we first glimpse her as a "damsel" of 16, at the beginning of this "tale in two parts," to the end of the novel, when we see her as a young woman of thirty, at the frontier of moral and spiritual recovery. *Chance* portrays her emotional and spiritual condition, covering a period of fourteen years, as it changes from one of spiritual impossibility to spiritual possibility, whatever the severe tribulations that she must undergo on the road to recovery, and whatever the profound costs of this recovery are in terms of the severe personal losses and the damages that she inevitably has to overcome, both in the life of "earthly things" and in the "sea-life" to which she is finally exposed, as she moves from her most troubled state of mind in contemplating suicide, into a problematic marriage and all of its radical consequences.

This movement is one that depicts the assault on innocence, the darkness of evil, the glimmer of self-understanding, and the bright rays of light that slowly illuminate her place in and view of the world. Moral darkness transforms into moral lucidity, with the possibility of love slowly transcending both the cruel absence of love and the loss of soul caused by human beings who harbor "unprincipled notions."

How does one's inner world survive the assaults of the outer world? How are we to redeem virtue and truth from a world of scepticism and cynicism, with its sham preconceptions and doctrines? Indeed, in *Chance* we discern an emerging confrontation between the forces of light and darkness, how it develops and how it culminates. The battle is between the forces of life and anti-life, between affirmation and denial. Moral warfare is in this novel a continuing preoccupation with Conrad.

The popular (and commercial) success of this novel—a distinctly English and post-Edwardian novel in manners and in personages—can in no way diminish the novel's seriousness of purpose and idea. No resolution of the moral struggle can be achieved without hard work invariably attended by misfortune, misunderstanding, misjudgment, misinterpretation. Indeed, none of Conrad's fictive characters here can be approached in simplistic or reductionist terms. Human interrelationships are both too intricate and too vulnerable to allow for superficial or one-dimensional analysis. They require careful probing if they are to have meaning for the reader. In

Chance, Conrad's exploration of the emotions is revealing, however murky and exasperating they happen to be.

There is no encapsulating symbolism in *Chance* that helps to place or to historicize the main constituents of the story. It is the inner terrain that is under full scrutiny; emotional aberrations and ambiguities, as these not only mirror the human motives, hopes and actions, but also affect both the lives and the personal relations between men and women, are focused on with a sustained force of perception. Events and scenes transpire on land and sea, but without any singular characteristic that has a memorable influence on the fate of any one individual. In fact, the world of nature has a perfunctory role to play in the lives of the novel's people. Conrad makes no special effort to paint for the reader some definitive seascape or cityscape which objectifies a particular condition, and which augments and deepens the meaning of the story. If anything, the physicality of the outer world in *Chance* has a neutral quality about it, and is of secondary importance to what Conrad is finally seeking to uncover in the innermost depths of relations.

Conrad's concentration is essentially cerebral in *Chance*. He largely eschews dramatic imagery in the form of a life-threatening typhoon, or of a military revolt, or of a political conspiracy in their consequential terrors to the community and to the soul. The language he employs in the novel is tempered and generally lacks the magic of phrase that characterizes the action scenes in his other novels. Even Conrad's use of Charles Marlow, who is variously described as an "auditor-narrator," a "born observer," a "reciter" in his fifties, and whose role is joined and enlarged by an anonymous outer narrator, an "interlocutor," in reconstructing the story of *Chance* as it filtered through multi-layered consciousnesses, underlines a kind of indirection in pulling together the story's fragments. That Marlow describes himself as "an investigator—a man of deductions"—calls attention to the cerebral orientation of the novel, and to the constituents of Conrad's narrative technique, what Henry James termed the "combined eccentricities of recital."[2]

The cerebral and the investigative aspects of *Chance* are reflected in the two successive parts of the novel, "The Damsel" and "The Knight," and in Conrad's matter-of-fact introduction of chapter headings, the first chapter entitled "Young Powell and His Chance," and the concluding chapter,

---

[2]See *Marlow*, ed. Harold Bloom (New York, 1992) 37-40, 43-44.

"A Moonless Night." In this novel, then, Conrad is inviting the reader to participate in the narrative process, diagnosing the "facts" of the story, and, in the end, to interpret and to judge its moral ramifications.

Lives are obviously on trial in this novel, and the reader is asked to weigh the attitudes, beliefs, conduct, and decisions that define the particular worth of character and the signs of its blind fate, or chance. This process is a cumulative one that expects the reader's involvement in "the recreation of vision" and also his rational appraisal of its content as it is rendered in specific interacting and unfolding scenes that, in effect, provide evidence for a verdict to be finally announced in a morally responsible way. The geometric pattern of the novel's content lends itself to the kind of discriminating reason the reader must appeal to in registering the factual information being conveyed. Ultimately the reader is separating fact from fiction in the "case" as he perceives its buildup, listens to the testimony, and assesses the people and the places that embody actions and outcomes. In this respect, Conrad is himself not concerned with the resolution of the novel's story line, but with the presentation to the reader of a particular "transaction" that requires analysis and judgment to bring closure.

Chance, some critics claim, is an example of Conrad's later fiction, published after *Under Western Eyes* (1911), which shows a decline of his imaginative genius and, in especial, a downturn in his thematic acuteness and craft. Such criticism no doubt is ignited by a novel that presents multiple points of view and combs states of consciousness in a more cerebral way, but that also relies on psychological realism and social observation as much as did his earlier fiction. One perceptive critic, in this connection, rightly stresses that a novel like *Chance* illustrates more how men and women struggle for meaning in an "amoral cosmos" than it argues for "a system of values."[3] The distinction made here is important in estimating the literary worth of *Chance*. One must be ready, then, to tackle this novel from a different literary and technical perspective, and to be willing to weigh the moral ideas of *Chance* in a less dramatic but equally demanding psychological process, in which mind and intellect encounter particular ideas about human passion, sexuality, and personal relations in all their tensions.

It should be remembered that *Chance* follows three political novels; that, in Daniel R. Schwartz's insightful observation, it further "sustains and

---

[3]Daniel R. Schwartz, "The Continuity of Conrad's Later Novels," in *Conrad Revisited: Essays for the Eighties* (Tuscaloosa AL, 1985) 151ff.

intensifies the stress on private life and passionate love as the only alternatives to a world threatened by materialism, political ideology, and uncontrollable historical forces."[4] Here, Conrad's implicit moral preoccupations are embodied in their passional expressions and realities; in short, they are given their respective human specificities in direct relation to "the curse of consciousness" that Conrad saw as an overarching human spectacle. If anything this novel heightens the human equation, but in a more narrowing context. There are deeper soundings of and penetrations into the human psyche, and a bolder willingness on the novelist's part to uncover personal motives and behavior to their ultimate degree. In some ways, in fact, much more is going on, inwardly, than in the earlier novels as distinguished by their outward melodramatic elements. The journey of discovery in *Chance* has a vertical destination, and it is less prophetic in its orientation and less flamboyant, or dramatic, in its rhetoric. Panorama and spirit of place are much less evident, or even memorable, in *Chance*; are even secondary to Conrad's major moral concern (and to the methods of addressing and recreating the very urgency of that concern) in this novel.

A certain creative fortitude finally characterizes Conrad's vision of human existence and meaning in *Chance*, and simultaneously impels the deliberation and the articulation of the moral constituents of his vision. To be sure, the framework of that vision may be structurally and technically a surprising departure from Conradian literary norms. In *Chance*, thus, an added technical and metaphysical dimension is manifest, uniting as it does the intelligence and the maturity of Conrad's vision as an artist. This novel, as such, marks a higher stage in the building of his moral imagination as it is now significantly enlarged and enriched by a ratiocinative thrust.

Conrad is himself profoundly aware of what precisely he is doing in this novel when he states in his "Author's Note": "But every subject in the region of intellect and emotion must have a morality of its own if it is treated at all sincerely. . . . " He goes on to say that he has on occasion perhaps sinned against matters of taste, but he also insists that he has not sinned against those "basic feelings and elementary convictions which make life possible to the mass of mankind and, by establishing a standard of judgment, set their idealism free to look for plainer ways, for higher feelings, for deeper purposes." *Chance* advances to a new level the intent

---

[4]Ibid., 163.

of these words, even as it remains loyal to Conrad's aim as an artist who unveils "the strangeness of the deeper truth."

II

From beginning to end, *Chance* concentrates on Flora de Barral's life. Even when she is not actually present in the text, as in the very first chapter, the figures we meet, and the places and objects we see, are there for the purpose of unveiling the story of her life. She is both the commanding presence, and the inclusive concern, and the consuming interest in the novel. The value of *Chance* as a novel finally depends on how successful Conrad is in his linear development of Flora's life and fate. Everything in the novel points to her, everything climaxes around her. *Chance* could have easily been titled *Flora*. The characters we meet in it, including the various narrators, the locales of the events as they occur, and the actions, big and small, that transpire here, as well as the central and defining ideas that inhere in the novel's total structure, have their very origin and reasons for existence in Flora's persona.

Without Flora, everything else, and everyone, would have no meaning and no validity. Her personal and moral power over the novel is astonishing, and unless we recognize the dynamic of this power we fail to grasp the novel's technical audacity. What ultimately characterizes Conrad's imaginative achievement in *Chance*, what gives it its uniqueness, in a line of continuity but also in intersecting lines, is the nature of the challenge that Conrad throws out to his readers. Unless readers, and critics, are up to this challenge, of meaning and interpretation, and unless they are willing to take, with Conrad, a leap of imagination, *Chance* will irritate and perhaps even offend their literary sensibility. Conrad perseveres here in his mission as a novelist who "is a historian, the preserver, the keeper, the expounder of human experience."

It is an elderly and retired Marlow, "who in his time had followed the sea," who, as one of the several narrators, first introduces the reader to Flora de Barrel as a young girl, recalling years later how he chanced to see her from below a high quarry he was passing. She was walking close to the edge of the quarry, "which rose a sheer hundred feet," and was in considerable danger: "At the sound of his voice she started back and retreated out of his sight amongst some young Scotch firs growing near the very brink of the precipice." Marlow was introduced to Flora only the day before the incident, at the round tea-table of a country cottage of his acquaintances, John and Zoe Fyne, "a good, stupid, earnest couple" who had befriended this obviously unhappy girl.

It is Marlow who originally provides the physical portrait of Flora: "Her hair was nearly black, her eyes blue, deeply shaded by long dark eyelashes. . . . her chin was fine, somehow pointed." He complains to the girl about her "reckless proceedings," which could lead to her death. "Had she given occasion for a coroner's inquest the verdict would have been suicide, with the implication of unhappy love." Her reply to Marlow, as he struggles to understand the reasons for her folly, is ominous: "She retorted that once one was dead, what horrid people thought of one did not matter." For Marlow this is a moment of sudden illumination: "I perceived then that her thick eyelashes were wet. This surprised me. . . . She looked unhappy. . . . The clouded brow, the pained mouth, the vague fixed glance! A victim."

Marlow's recollection is a kind of prelude that prepares a reader for what will take place in the life of Flora, and also for the consequences that "a life of moral anguish" both objectifies and entails. That Marlow more or less rescues the girl from suicide underlines the salvational theme of *Chance* that is consonant with the possibility of moral recovery. From the very start, then, we discern in Flora a hapless victim of fate. She is the daughter and only child of de Barral, a London financier who promised ten per cent dividends on all deposits made in his "Thrift and Independence Aid Association." Having lent the moneys he received "without system, plan, foresight or judgment," he discovered that his business operations were collapsing abysmally as hundreds of naive and unsuspecting depositors lost their money.

We learn that de Barral, incredibly inept in his financial dealings, attracted "all sorts of swindlers, adventurers, visionaries, and even lunatics." He himself is not a conscious charlatan, but rather a man who, because of "his unimaginative stupidity," lends himself to "fantastic schemes." During the bankruptcy proceedings and the criminal prosecution, he is pitiable figure: "There was something perfect in his consistent mediocrity. His very vanity seemed to miss the gratification of even the mere show of power." After "a whole week of industrious sittings," de Barral, who had once "juggled with accounts, cooked balance sheets, had gathered in deposits months after he ought to have known himself to be hopelessly insolvent," was "to earn for himself seven years' penal servitude."

De Barral's function in *Chance* is not to be glossed over or underestimated; his power of presence and influence pervades the entire novel and affects the moral fate of the novel's characters. At first, it seems, de Barral is a kind of burlesque figure, at times even laughable in his absurdity, in his folly, in his self-conceit and self-delusion. But he is also extraordinarily transparent in his deficiencies and irresponsibility, which have grave results in the novel's economy and ethos. Above all, it is in de Barral himself that the reader discovers the special difficulties of Flora's formative years. In fact, de Barral personifies the very pattern of the obstacles and disadvantages that Flora has to overcome if her life is to take on a moral shape. In a deep sense, de Barral is the shadow that, in Flora's life, falls between appearance and reality. Both as husband of a very decent woman and as father of an only child, de Barral is notoriously indifferent and selfish. He has "packed off" his wife and daughter to live "in a big stone mansion with mullioned windows in a large damp park, called the Priory," as he looks after his business interests in London. While in "exile," his wife dies, "from neglect, absolutely from neglect, rather unexpectedly and without any fuss."

De Barral, we learn, managed to go to the funeral—he "was extremely cut up, and holding the child by the hand wept bitterly, at the side of the grave." But he immediately returned to London on "the half-past five fast train," leaving Flora alone with a middle-aged governess, who "despised" Mrs. de Barral, "didn't care for the child a bit," and "bullied" de Barral to take a new "splendidly furnished house in the most expensive part of Brighton for them." For the most part, young Flora continues to live her life in exile, though her father "now and then ran down for a weekend, with a trunk full of exquisite sweets and with his hat full of money." The sociology of Flora's early familial experiences is, then, something that must be kept in mind, for it plays a profound role in how she comes to perceive herself, how vulnerable she is in the world into which she has been thrown, and in which its "horrors" seem almost to swallow her.

Conrad depicts Flora's circumstances in human and not clinical detail, as he describes the "accidents" that occur in her life, or as Marlow expresses it: "By accident I mean that which happens blindly and without intelligent design." "The vagaries of fate" in Flora's life are crucial, and Conrad draws them both incisively and insightfully, in unraveling the meaning of her life's story in its parts and whole. His aim is to reveal Flora to the reader even as she reveals herself to herself in the course of the novel.

Marlow happens to meet the Fynes and their three daughters in the country, "in their holiday time." We find that Mrs. Fyne is the center of the attention of various young and pretty girls, including Flora, who would come to stay with her in the cottage: "They treated her with admiring deference. She answered to some need of theirs. They sat at her feet. They were like disciples." Mrs. Fyne has a "voluntary mission": "to befriend, counsel, and guide young girls of all sorts on the path to life." We learn, too, that Mrs. Fyne is the "domestic slave-daughter" of Carleon Anthony, a respected poet, "a savage sentimentalist," but also a tyrannical husband and father ("who, by the way, wore out two women without any satisfaction to himself, because they did not come up to his supra-refined standard of the delicacy which is so perceptible in his verse"). Mrs. Fyne is also the older sister of Captain Roderick Anthony ("a good soul"), who becomes the "master of the *Ferndale*," and who eventually will become Flora's husband.

Both of the poet's children had escaped from "bondage" to their father, the rebellious daughter "by throwing herself into the arms, the muscular arms, of the pedestrian Fyne," "a good little man in the Civil Service," and the contemplative brother by running away and, "as if disgusted with the amenities of civilization," throwing "himself, figuratively speaking, into the sea." The sailor-brother is a gentle, retiring, shy man, devoted to his "calling" as a merchant-sailor, distrustful of "shore people" and "the wickedness of the solid world surrounded by the salt, uncorruptible waters." He was to choose, in short, to live "a life of solitude and silence—and desire."

Mrs. Fyne, whose "self-possession" and "neutral manner" strike Marlow as that of a governess, "had adopted that cool, detached manner to meet her gifted father's outbreaks of temper." Not surprisingly, she concocts an "individualist women-doctrine, naively unscrupulous," and is the author of a "sort of handbook for women with grievances (and all women had them), a sort of compendious theory and practice of feminine free morality." Mrs. Fyne does "not want women to be women. Her theory was that they should turn themselves into unscrupulous sexless nuisances. An offended theorist dwelt in her bosom somewhere." Her role in Flora's life will be seen to be fateful, in its own way no less fateful than her father's role: "It was as if the forehead of Flora de Barral were marked. Was the girl born to be a victim; to be always disliked and crushed as if she were too fine for this world? Or too luckless—since that also is often counted as sin."

In the main, Marlow, by putting together and recounting *verbatim* the happenings in the novel, as these in turn have been variously but not sequentially reported years later to him in fragments by acquaintances, such as Charles Powell, at one time the second officer of the *Ferndale*, and by other unnamed people, provides us with a narrative unity, and thus enables us to form a conclusive picture of Flora's victimhood and also, finally, her rescue and recovery.

Another woman who plays a role in Flora's life is an "amazing governess," whose first name, Eliza, is only used. That Conrad devotes an entire chapter, "The Governess," to her alerts us to her significance in the novel. For more than five years this governess was to be in charge of young Flora. We meet the governess being joined, in the house in Brighton, by a "supposed" nephew, Charley, who has just come from London unexpectedly to relate to Flora's governess the news of the Great de Barral's imminent "cataclysm." The governess, finally learning of de Barral's complete fall, will now brutally abandon her charge and abscond, with all the money cashed from the checking account, which de Barral had in her name, from de Barral's Brighton mansion. The impact on Flora of her father's "financial crash" will be incalculable, to be compounded by the governess's full-scale desertion.

The governess personifies ultimate wickedness, and is devoid of either compassion or sincerity. She is still another powerful figure in Conrad's hall of evil ones. She represents unmitigating hatred and tenacity, desperately clinging "to her last infatuation for that graceless young scamp." She is a woman without illusion, hard, calculating, filled with hatred, without a shred of decency. Conrad portrays her actions in the most terrifying terms, as faithfully reported to Marlow by Mr. Fyne, who with his wife, who had known de Barral's late wife, lived in apartments "a few doors down on the opposite side of the street" while on a week's holiday in Brighton, and who, to the governess's horror, were monitoring the "moral dangers" menacing the "unlucky" and "defenceless" Flora. The description of conditions in the de Barral house is harrowing in its details, underlining the awful loss of security facing Flora during her last meeting with the governess and Charley.

Conrad takes special pains to show just how distressing is the final encounter in the drawing room between Flora and Eliza. The governess's features and bearing alarm Flora: "There was something like an emanation of evil from her face. . . . " The buildup of "the force of the shock in the intuitive perception" of danger on the girl's part is especially evident—"she had received suddenly the feeling of being personally attacked." This episode is for Flora fraught with danger; it is as if her very existence is about to be destroyed. Conrad's deep critical insights into adolescent psychology highlight this entire episode in Flora's formative years. Parts of this story are actually reported years afterward by Mrs. Fyne to Flora, who could never forget its terrors—"it remained like a mark on her soul, a sort of mystic wound, to be contemplated, to be meditated over." The governess's "venomous abuse" of Flora at this point has an almost incredible demonic verbal thrust that goes to the depths of her being. Cruelty can be felt here as the governess directs her "accumulated resentment, the infinite hatred of all these unrelieved years," on a helpless young girl, "a frail and passive vessel" into which to pour "miserable revenge."

To the governess, Flora is "in heart, mind, manner and appearance an utterly common and insipid figure," even though the girl can hardly comprehend the causes of "the violence of the attack." The governess's diatribe is almost serpentine in its traits, as Flora's later recollection indicates: "She pushed her face so near mine and her teeth looked as though she wanted to bite me. Her eyes seemed to have become quite dry, hard and small in a lot of horrible wrinkles." The scene has dramatic momentum, climaxing at the point when the governess, now in the throes of "sadistic pleasure," calls the girl "the child of a cheat and a swindler," adding almost immediately after Flora's fervent protest ("You mustn't speak like this of papa!"): "You shall hear it and you shall read it—and then you will know whose daughter you are. . . . He's nothing but a thief . . . this father of yours." Horrified and fearful, Flora "sat up suddenly with the wild staring expression of being choked by invisible fingers on her throat and yet horribly pale."

This is an astonishing scene, and one of Conrad's most memorable as it proceeds to a conclusion of spent emotions: "The end came in the abomination of desolation of the child's miserable cry for help: 'Charley! Charley!' coming from her throat in hidden gasping efforts." The youthful paramour, hitherto "motionless and dumb," seeming at last to realize the magnitude of the danger that a screaming, out-of-control woman poses to Flora, mercifully intervenes, seizes the woman by the arm, and says commandingly, "Come away, Eliza." And instantly, the child was to see the two of them, "close together and remote, near the door, gone through the door, which she neither heard nor saw being opened or shut. But it was shut. Oh yes, it was shut." Eliza and Charley will no longer appear in the novel, or in Flora's life, but the damage to her soul will endure in "that Book of Destiny [that] has been written up from the beginning to the last page."

On the evening of the next day, an elderly man unexpectedly comes to fetch Flora from her temporary sanctuary with the Fynes in their hotel sitting-room, to which she had fled. This "man in black" was a cousin of de

Barral, who had earlier asked him to take the girl from the Fynes and to give her house-room for a time in his family. This "unforeseen but perfectly authorized guardian," perceived by the Fynes as a respectable but totally vulgar member of the lower middle classes, clearly believes that it is worth rescuing Flora in the event that the failed financier had somehow managed to hang on to an estate in the country and a comfortable income.

The very next day, in the afternoon, de Barral's cousin takes Flora, now at the age of sixteen, who "no longer looked a child," away with him to another area to begin there still another sad phase in her life. Flora's life in the cousin's household "down Limehouse way" in London's East End, was to be a no less incredible "moral savagery." In the new household she suffers harsh insults at the hands of that "grubbing lot," with their repeated "importunities, insolence and exigencies." Here, once again, she "had her most secret feelings lacerated, had obtained a view of the utmost baseness to which common human nature can descend."

And again, one cold and drizzly night, Flora flees to the Fynes's house in London; and again de Barral's relative turns up one morning to interpose "his authority for the protection of the girl." The "beastly relative" was thus stubbornly clinging to his belief "that de Barral has got some plunder put away somewhere," and would make a claim on the "convict" once he was released from prison on the strength of his having looked after Flora. The picture of Flora being "always surrounded by treachery and lies stifling every better impulse, every inspiration of her soul to trust and to love," is consistently reinforced in the entire novel. Before another year is out, we behold Flora once again at the Fynes's door, having been evicted by her relative, who no doubt had given up hope of staking any "claim" on de Barral's vanished fortune. The Fynes now make arrangements with "a certain old lady" in Bournemouth to care for Flora "in the quality of reader and companion." But she does not find the girl at all "cheerful" and the "strain" of this prompts her to give up on Flora.

Next comes another short episode in Flora's dreary odyssey, when the Fynes arrange for her to stay with a well-to-do German family in Hamburg. The husband, it appears, "wanted to be loved," no less than the Bournemouth old lady, and "he set about his sinister enterprise" to deceive an innocent Flora about his amorous purposes, discovered by the German's wife, who angrily reproaches the girl for bringing "dishonor to my home." Flora, on a rainy winter evening, is "handed bag and baggage on board a steamer for London." Her plight finds her "scared as near as possible into hysterics," with even "the shades of death gathering round the moral weariness of bewildering thinking which makes the idea of nonexistence welcome so often to the young." Flora returns to the safety of the Fyne household, there to become a part of Mrs. Fyne's circle of "girl-friends," but not a disciple of the latter's feminist "salad of unprincipled notions."

It is during this particular period that Captain Anthony, now a man of thirty-five, who happens to be visiting his sister in the summer cottage in the country, becomes infatuated with Flora, whom he met accidentally. (The girl had been earlier introduced to Marlow simply as "Miss Smith.") Mrs. Fyne has also never really been comfortable with her; at no time did she think of Flora as being particularly charming or sympathetic. While observing the budding relationship between Flora and her brother, Mrs. Fyne was distressed by its "duplicity"—and by Flora's "ingratitude." The possibility of their marrying clearly bothered Mrs. Fyne, who cannot hide her discomfort with the idea that a "girl-friend" will eventually run off with her sailor-brother. " 'You see, Mr. Marlow,' she said in an unexpectedly confidential tone, 'they are so utterly unsuited for each other.' " Ultimately, then, what is also bothering her is the idea of "[t]he purloining of the son of the poet-tyrant by the daughter of the financier-convict."

When Captain Anthony does run off with Flora, Mrs. Fyne, abetted by her husband, is intent on "thrusting a stick in the spokes of another woman's wheel." She will, therefore, send her husband to London on such a destructive mission; she will, in short, add considerably to Flora's personal and emotional crisis. She personifies, then, yet another major danger to Flora in her plan to keep two people apart, even after Flora has followed Captain Anthony to London within forty-eight hours of his departure. Though Mrs. Fyne "had not much use for her brother," she was intent on deterring him from marriage to Flora. "What your wife cannot tolerate in this affair," Marlow says to Mr. Fyne, "is Miss de Barral being what she is. . . . In other words, that she can't forgive Miss de Barral for being a woman and behaving like a woman." She thus presents an insidious threat to Flora's future happiness, and is still another hurdle for the girl to jump over. Following his wife's wishes, Fyne goes to the Eastern Hotel, in London, for the purpose of seeing Captain Anthony, before the latter is joined by Flora on their way to see the docked *Ferndale*. In a sense, Fyne is her emissary, her "appointed" spokesman for "her extreme theoretical position," as it is defined in her "inflammatory book." Again, it is Marlow, whose shout had earlier checked Flora in her suicide attempt, who happens to see her "on the pavement," making her way to meet Captain Anthony.

The meeting, "on the pavement," between Marlow and Flora, served to bring together two "strangers," "who had dealt with the most intimate and final subjects, the subject of death"—and now, "on the pavement," in front of the hotel, the "subject of marriage." This scene in the London street, "in the odious uproar of that wide roadway thronged with heavy carts," is an ominous encounter, and helps to deepen the complexity of Flora's circumstances and the impediments she faces in the context of personal relations, and specifically her relation to the chivalrous and idealistic Roderick Anthony, who first sees Flora at the Fynes's cottage and thinks that this was "a possible woman." The relation between them blossoms during long walks and discussions; she, alienated from life, is instinctively drawn to a man who is "a confirmed enemy of life on shore."

In her misery the captain, who "was gentleness itself," sees his opportunity—"It gave him the feeling that if only he could get hold of her, no woman would belong to him so completely as this woman." The passion they both experience marks a new tempo in Conrad's fiction, in which emotions are generally muted. The Flora we observe here being "condemned to a degrading sort of poverty" had implanted in her "a lasting doubt, an ineradicable suspicion of herself and others." Her view, then, of forming an attachment to another human being has been much besmirched by the circumstances of her life. In accepting Captain Anthony's proposal to marry him it is clear that she sees in her decision a golden opportunity to escape from a life of "horrors."

Flora's favorable response to the captain, she informs Mrs. Fyne in a confessional letter of "eight pages of close writing," reflects in some ways the tenuous impingement of Mrs. Fyne's feminist views. In this "famous letter" she writes that she does not love the sailor-brother, that she was "unscrupulous" in accepting his offer of marriage, that what she did was in "self-defence." The letter further confirms Flora's troubled state of mind, and also indicates her desperation in the face of probable annihilation. Mr. Fyne, "the emissary of an order of things which stops at the edge of the sea," clearly fails in his mission once Flora has finally entered the hotel. Flora and Captain Anthony will indeed marry, and Flora in fact will soon meet her convict-father, having served his prison sentence, at the jail door: "They mean to drag him along with them on board the ship straight away. Rescue work."

III

The chapter "On the Pavement" concludes the first part of the novel, "The Damsel"; the second and shorter part, "The Knight," relates the outcome of the "Rescue Work." In this part, the story of Flora de Barral, given interruptedly in stages, with the bits of disconnected statements pieced together by Marlow, attains moral resolution. *Chance* is not only about Flora's defeats or about her steadfastness and courage in the face of disastrous personal circumstances. It also tells the story of Captain Anthony, for whom Conrad had "a natural liking," as he informs the reader in his "Author's Note." Though Conrad was sympathetic towards Flora, he found it difficult to continue with her story: "I failed at first to get hold of her." The character of the captain, as Conrad was to envision its place in the story, helped him to overcome the "hesitation" and the "indecision" that impeded his compositional task: "I said to myself that if that man was so determined to embrace a 'wisp of mist' the best thing for me was to join him in that eminently practical and praiseworthy adventure. I simply followed Captain Anthony." In the end, then, *Chance* is about the power of determination, how it flickers, develops, and is grasped in a world of "mere chance . . . manifesting itself often in delicate forms such for instance as the charm, true or illusory, of a human being."

Moral subtleties are an organic facet of this novel and must be discerned if *Chance* and its creative and critical worth are to be fully appreciated. This is still another major novel of Conrad's that presents a moral challenge to the reader, and that enlists the reader in the pursuit of a moral virtue, but without reducing that pursuit to a formulaic context. It is a pursuit of what Conrad himself speaks of as the "adventure" "to put one's finger on the imponderable." *Chance* renders this adventure in all of its twists and turns, its disconnections, perplexities, contradictions. The narrative process in *Chance*, the fusion of content and technique, as Crankshaw reminds us, is one in which "[a]ll things work together for good"—a process which produces the "super-augmentation of effect."[5] It is precisely within this process in *Chance* that Conrad's moral concerns are to be noticed as they transform into moral values.

The second part of *Chance* depicts significant changes in human relationships, especially as these changes affect Captain Anthony. No longer

---

[5]Page 51.

is his command of the *Ferndale* his main priority as he assumes his marital responsibility to Flora. His chief mate and "jealously devoted subordinate," Mr. Franklin, resents Mrs. Anthony's presence aboard ship, and is also perturbed by the presence of Flora's father, "Mr. Smith." Young Charles Powell, who had taken a position as the ship's second officer (not long after passing his seamanship examination), suddenly asked to replace Mr. Mathews, the officer badly injured in a freak accident just prior to the departure of the *Ferndale*, also serves as a narrative speaker who recalls events during and after the years of Flora's marriage to Captain Anthony. These events take place, in the course of the *Ferndale*'s several voyages, over a period of years.

The living arrangements of the newly married couple are rather unusual, with the private part of a long saloon, "consecrated to the exclusiveness of Captain Anthony's married life . . . cut off from the rest of that forbidden space by a pair of heavy curtains." From the skylight seat on deck Powell was able to follow and observe the captain's movements. His "peeping" was in some ways spurred by Mr. Franklin's cynical talk so as to raise "a sort of unhealthy curiosity which did away . . . with all the restraints of common decency." What is made clear here is that the marriage between Flora and Anthony is in part the result of the captain's feelings of pity and kindness for Flora, and his "rescue" of her; the reader is made equally aware of "the secret of the situation," of an unconsummated marriage that is based on "judicious reticences."

Flora's original position among "the shore people" is essentially no less difficult than what it is now: "For under a cloud Flora de Barral was fated to be even at sea." Clearly, she has to contend with the problematic aspects of her marriage, with caring for her old father whom she has taken with her on the *Ferndale*, with the lingering memories of her past, and now with the suspicion and the hostility of the members of the crew ("the old lot"): "They had the funny, regretful glances, intonations, nods of men who had seen other, better times." (It is no small irony, too, that during one of its voyages, the *Ferndale* is transporting dynamite in cases and blasting powder in barrels.) Indeed, de Barral's presence on the ship has a way of continuing Flora's problems beyond "the wickedness of the solid world."

Flora and her father introduce a foreign element in the lives of the crew, jarring the equilibrium of the ship's passage and the accustomed routine at sea. Mr. Franklin, for one, is aggrieved that he has been "chucked out of the saloon as if I weren't good enough to sit down with that woman." He also speaks for other "aggrieved" members of the crew when he says to an inexperienced and innocent Powell: "And of course you haven't known the ship as she used to be. She was more than a home to a man. She was not like any other ship; and Captain Anthony was not like any other master to sail with. . . . there was never anything to worry about." Illusions are confronted boldly in *Chance*; life on the *Ferndale*, we come to realize, is no "fairy-tale." Indeed, it is young Powell who personifies the brush with reality when for the first time he beholds Mrs. Anthony, who in her person upsets his "preconceived ideal" of a captain's wife—"a girl where your average mediocre imagination had placed a comparatively old woman": "It was a sort of moral upset as though he had discovered a case of abduction or something as surprising as that." "Shock" and "astonishment" thus characterize Powell's first view on the *Ferndale* of Flora and her father.

In *Chance* Conrad once again depicts how the power of illusion comes to an end in contact with reality, as instanced in Powell's reactions to the "old gentleman" and his daughter ("queer passengers"). The encounter, particularly with de Barral, "becoming so suddenly articulate in a darkening universe," is especially illuminating for Powell; Conrad captures the prescient quality of the scene in these words: "[I]t was distinctly at that moment that he became aware of something unusual not only in this encounter but generally around him, about everybody, in the atmosphere."

Powell's sense of awareness is heightened by his brief conversation with the old man—it has to do with the second mate Powell had replaced, an elderly man, according to de Barral, who was taken to hospital, "Possibly about to die. . . . And perhaps glad enough to die." Young Powell, it should be recalled, is startled at this suggestion, "which sounded confidential and blood-curdling in the dusk." A sort of friendship was to develop between de Barral and Powell, with the latter at times assisting the infirm old man, "always limping," whom the crew members, including Anthony himself, "shunned . . . as though he had been the devil."

The presence of Flora's father on the *Ferndale* is cast in dark and ominous tones and colors, and it is as if a damaged soul has transferred from a shore prison to a sea prison, to which an enduring Flora ("Women can stand anything"), on an errand of mercy, brought her father in a cab heading to the dock on the day he was released from jail. Unlike Flora, who remained totally loyal to her father—even "in the distrust of herself and of others she looked for love, any kind of love, as women will,"—her father was to harbor spiteful feelings nourished by his captivity in prison ("the shutting up with its mental suggestions of bang, snap, crash and the empty silence outside"): "Old pains keep on gnawing at your heart, old desires, old deceptions, old dreams, assailing you in the dead stillness of your life." Her father seems a different human being to Flora, shocked and frightened by "the close look she took at his face," and sensing a profound change now affecting their relationship: "Yes, there was something between them, something hard and impalpable, the ghost of these high walls."

Their reunion is not altogether a happy one, and when they do embrace in the cab it seems awkward and fumbling: "She hid her face on his breast. It was as though she were pressing a stone. . . . with those two people as far apart as they could get from each other, in opposite corners." The scene is a portentous one, heralding as it does still another obstacle put in Flora's way to love and trust in life. Her own fleeting recollections of "bewildering difficulties and humiliations" seem to haunt and hamper any genuine appreciation of consummate joy. That she also now tells her father of her recent marriage to Captain Anthony presents, simultaneously, a profound difficulty, to the news of which he reacts with incomprehension. The unexpected news "seemed to stick in his throat. In strangled low tones he cried out, 'You—married? You, Flora! When? Married! What for? Who to? Married!' "

De Barral here personifies the negatives of pride, bitterness, disillusion—and, above all, the selfishness of one who simply cannot stand the thought of his daughter not maintaining filial loyalty to him alone. His is the selfishness of one who cannot really perceive the innermost feelings, the longings, of a woman who "had lived a life so starved of all feeling that this [father-daughter intimacy] was no longer enough for her"—and who increasingly found it difficult "to get away from life's betrayals." In his attitude he shows how much he is a slave of a preconceived idea: "I am the great Mr. de Barral . . . and I have my little girl. I wanted nobody and I have never had anybody." He will not, it is quite clear, accept Flora's husband Anthony (who, he assumes, is "perhaps a fool," "anyway, not good enough"; "What is he? Where did he spring from?")

Out of pity and remorse Flora seeks to save her father in a future she has arranged—"to sail away from this abominable world of treacheries, and scorns and envies and lies, away, away over the blue sea, the sure, the inaccessible, the uncontaminated and spacious refuge for wounded souls." In the confines of the cab an outraged de Barral responds to Flora's "argument of refuge" with "an instinctive panic" as he struggled to get out. Unhesitantly she was able to restrain the frail old man and to keep him there resolutely until they arrived at the docks. Obstinate in his resistance, he pushes Flora away from him, her head striking the side of the cab: "All the warmth went out of her emotion. The very last tears turned cold on her cheek." Exhausted and dejected, they both at last board the *Ferndale*: "But he carried in his heart the confused pain of dismay and affection, of involuntary repulsion and pity. Very much like his daughter. Only in addition he felt a furious jealousy of the man [Captain Anthony] he was going to see."

De Barral's attitude, solidified by his penal servitude, is defined by a paternal sense of ownership of Flora, who was the "only thing, the one point where his thought found a resting-place, for years. She was the only outlet for his imagination." Captain Anthony confronts the problem of "Mr. Smith"—"I am here under protest," he declares—with the simplicity of a man who entertains no meannesses and makes no mean reservations. Conrad emphasizes here the sharp differences in character between the two men. The father's character is invariably one-dimensional; he is unwavering in his egoism, his fixed ideas, his self-righteousness. While in the ship's state-room, "fitted especially to receive Mr. Smith," he comments to his daughter: "Mrs. Anthony, I can't bear the sight of the fellow." It is all too evident that the *Ferndale*'s approaching first voyage, before the one Powell was to join, would not be an easy one—for the couple, for de Barral, or for the crew, including the steward's wife, Mrs. Brown, who would attend to Flora's needs but who was also to be an object of the latter's dislike: "The most unrestful ship that ever sailed out of any port on earth. . . . unrestful in the sense . . . of an uneasy atmosphere disturbed by passions, jealousies, loves, hates and the troubles of transcendental good intentions. . . ." The first and short trip of the *Ferndale* to the Western Islands only—it was seven months in fact since "the liberation of the convict de Barral and his avatar into Mr. Smith"—emblematizes the terrible burden of tensions and "hidden fury" the *Ferndale* is carrying, especially as these are concentrated in Mr. de Barrel's unassuaging antagonism to Anthony—"he would never rest till he had 'got her away from that man.' "

It has, in fact, been little noted that "the great de Barral" is possessed by devils no less menacing than those that possess Flora's governess; that these two figures, in tandem, represent an evil difficult to defeat. This evil afflicts the *Ferndale*, possesses the ship's soul, threatens its moral balance. De Barral is both a continuity and a completion of the governess's diabolism; indeed, the father here is the evil waiting to erupt, and, throughout an entire chapter, he is painted in demonic detail by Conrad. De Barral is, in essence, a representative of diabolism, fraught with "duplicity," "a taciturn person as far back as she [Flora] remembered him best," with a "wincing twitch" of his mouth, "a scornful grimace as faint and faded and colourless as his whole stiff personality." He is the "stranger" with the new name of "Mr. Smith," released from his temporary bondage, a "liberated convict" free to poison the "world of waters." "With staring eyes and gasping mouth," changing his countenance at will, depending on the particular circumstances, he is [a] gentleman in a silk hat, darting wary glances." "How was one to deal with him?"

In the presence of Captain Anthony, "admirable in his earnestness, in his sincerity and also in his restraint," de Barral is quintessentially the "Adversary," inherently threatened by Anthony's nearness. He is "impervious to words, to facts, to inferences": "It would have been impossible to make him see his guilt or his folly—either by evidence or argument—if anybody had tried to argue." He is possessed by "awful and precise visions which nothing could dislodge." Even from his room can be heard "a sound of muttering and of faint thuds," which arrest Anthony's attention, his eyes "big with wonder": "It was extraordinary. 'He's talking to himself. . . . He seems to be thumping the bulkhead with his fists—or his head.' " Restlessly, de Barral looks forward anxiously to the time he can "save" his daughter from Anthony, "the man who had possessed himself of her. . . . while he, the father, was locked up." He believes Flora has "sold" herself to the captain, "the head jailor." At this point, the novel is manifestly saturated with the language of evil from which one cannot easily get away, any more than one can get away from undesirable relations ("bad enough on shore") beyond the shore world.

The *Ferndale* is like a ship of horrors; everything that has gone wrong on land is accentuated and solidified in the stillness and solitariness of the deep waters. De Barral's monomania exhibits the energy and the reach of evil, as Conrad focuses on its meanness and cruelty in the confines of the ship. The reader is made acutely aware of both the range of its afflictions and the power of its perpetrators—and of the unending moral warfare that it ignites. The interior of the ship, with its "magnificent accommodation," its "sumptuosity," its state of order—"everything in its place, even to the silver on the sideboard"—is certainly an impressive sight, but in the final analysis a deception. For it, too, has its own "heart of darkness," as it is signaled from the first day when Flora tours the *Ferndale* with Captain Anthony as her caressive guide and future husband. The very next day when he returns to the ship, the chief mate's reaction to the shipkeeper's description of the tour is one of instinctive scorn (for "something was wrong"): a prelude to strife in the approaching years and voyages. In some ways the *Ferndale* becomes a concentrated vision of hell, into the innermost chambers of which Conrad allows a reader to glimpse the abnormities of life, as these are unlocked and then unmasked in the process of time.

The vulnerability of the human situation is a constant in Conrad's fiction. Dangers come unannounced, suddenly and violently, darkening the human scene, and testing to the full the human capacity to endure. These dangers are often ladened with a secret meaning and provide an index to character and conduct; they help to illustrate a moral measure that affects the outer and the inner life the novelist is exploring, and that gives *Chance* its specificity of value and recognition in the context of emerging human relationships. One such episode that stands out takes place during young Powell's first voyage on the *Ferndale* as the ship is getting clear of the channel. The weather is gloomy and threatening, with "a dead head wind, blowing quite half a gale." It is about ten o'clock at night, with Powell alone on the poop, "in charge," "when amongst the white breaking seas, under the black sky, he made out the lights of a ship." He surmises that the approaching ship "will pass jolly close . . . heading straight for us." He is made especially uneasy by the thought that the tons of dynamite in the body of the *Ferndale* are "not the sort of cargo one thinks of with equanimity in connexion with a threatened explosion."

Immediately, then, forgetting the chief mate's remarks on the change in the location of the captain to the port side, Powell rushes to the starboard side of the ship, and shouts down on the cowl of the big ventilator for the captain to come on deck. "[H]e heard only a faint exclamation—then silence." The voice is Mrs. Anthony's. An alarmed Powell rushed to the ship's side and struck the blue light on the rail, but there was a misfire, further alarming him to the possibility of a fatal collision of both ships. At this point he does hear "the measured voice" of the captain on the deck telling him to fetch the flare-up kept inside the companion with a box of matches nearby. Again Powell is unsuccessful. Mrs. Anthony, who appears a little below him on the stairs, helps in lighting the flare-up. Then "He bolted out of the companion straight into his captain who took the flare from him and held it high above his head." The collision is thus avoided, but it is "a close shave," in the captain's own words.

This episode marks the first time that Powell was to get in touch with Flora, who is for him a "jolly girl." Somewhat later he learns from Franklin that the captain has gone below: "He was walking the deck when suddenly he laughed a little and made for the companion. Thought of something funny all at once." Powell is clearly shocked to learn that Captain Anthony "had laughed without visible cause on a certain night." It was then, too, while finishing his watch, that it occurs to young Powell's "unsophisticated mind that perhaps things are not what they are confidently expected to be; that it was possible that Captain Anthony was not a happy man. . . . that all was not well in that cabin, so unusually cut off from the rest of the ship. . . ."

The near collision of the *Ferndale* and another ship, as it is described in the third chapter of the second part, entitled "Devoted Servants—And the Light of a Flare," is immediately followed by the chapter "Anthony and Flora." In it we become privy to the "marital quarrel" of Anthony and Flora. We begin to learn more about the circumstances of their visible estrangement, thorough and rapid in the process of its decomposition at sea. Here we look into Anthony's heart, we contemplate his dreams and passions, and we more fully fathom his quality of character—his form of heroism which "wears the aspect of sublime delicacy." This chapter is eminently probing in its narrative reflections from different theoretical angles, examining Anthony's life as "a life of solitude and silence—and desire." His "violent conquest of Flora" is consonant with a passion that "matures slowly in the unexplored recesses of the heart," and that, finally "invading the whole man and subjugating all his faculties to its own unique end, may conduct him . . . to the brink of unfathomable dangers, to the limits of folly and madness, and death."

What exactly are the constituents of his love for Flora, born from pity and tenderness and generosity, and yet perhaps even akin to immense vanity? What prompts Anthony, following his awkward encounter with Fyne, in the hotel room, and apprised of Flora's damning letter to Mrs. Fyne, what prompts him to make up his mind to give her liberty on the *Ferndale*? Silently, as we see, they go on board "the honest ship," which he promises her will be "your home," and also her father's. ("He was ready to take old de Barral—the convict—on his daughter's valuation without the slightest reserve.") For her, however, Anthony's "madness of generosity" is a "new perfidy of life taking upon itself the form of magnanimity." Nobody, she believes, could ever love her for herself: "It was as that abominable governess had said. She was insignificant, contemptible."

If for Flora marriage initially was to signify a form of captivity, for Roderick Anthony it was meant for her salvation. His was "a special sort of exultation which seemed to take him by the throat like an enemy." Indeed, Roderick Anthony is denied felicity in marriage, for which he suffers: "He was not a common sort of lover; and he was punished for it as if Nature (which it is said abhors a vacuum) were so very conventional as to abhor every sort of exceptional conduct. Yet he accepts "an impossible existence" for himself and his wife, even as he accepts Fyne's testimony regarding Flora's rejection of him as specified in the letter to Mrs. Fyne. He is besieged by humiliation, even as Flora is resigned to being "a mere worthless object of pity": "both had taken a bite of the same bitter fruit."

IV

In the very last chapter of *Chance*, "A Moonless Night," it is Powell who has a central role; his recollections of the final happenings on the *Ferndale*, as passed on to Marlow, help to clarify the tale in its entirety, and also to provide a moral resolution. Some critics of *Chance* dismiss Conrad's method of presentation and especially his resolution as the direct failure of the novelist's reliance on the "large generalizations, the clichés, the vague rhetorical outbursts" that pervade the novel.[6] Such criticism, however, instances an unfairness to *Chance*, and also underlines impatience with what Conrad is at pains trying to do in it. In *Chance* Conrad is forcefully grappling with moral possibility, in the form of the effort, if not the sympathy, needed both to experience and to understand the moral progression of the distinct lines and dynamic forms that it takes in the soul-life, as it were.

This concluding chapter, it can be said, serves as Conrad's tribute to the power of moral possibility, epitomized in these words: "And the science of life consists in seizing every chance that presents itself." This sentence could be appropriately added to the epigraph, words from Sir Thomas Browne, on the title page: "Those that hold that all things are governed by Fortune had not erred, had they not persisted there." Here we find Powell, one moonless night, coming up, at eight o'clock, to take charge of the deck. Somewhat later, de Barral was also to come up to the deck, striking up a conversation with Powell, and noting in his usual enigmatic way that Flora has taken a liking to the second mate. He then returned to his room to go to bed, as Powell settled down to his regular duties as officer of the watch. Passing by the mizzen-mast, he noticed a coil of rope forgotten on the deck. Stooping to pick it up, he happened to look directly into the private part of the saloon "consecrated to the exclusiveness of Captain Anthony's married life." Fascinated by the scene below him, he watches the captain taking a

---

[6]Douglas Hewitt, *Conrad: A Reassessment* (Chester Springs PA, 1969) 99.

drink of brandy-and-water, and reading a history book in the cabin of the ship on a quiet night, before suddenly jumping up and walking away aft. Mr. Franklin's demeaning remarks, it is made clear, had aroused Powell's "unhealthy curiosity" and prompted him to "spy" on the captain, thus doing away "with all the restraints of common decency."

But Powell is not alone in "the highly incorrect occupation of watching the movements of Captain Anthony," for he discovers that there is still another watcher, one who has quietly separated the two curtains in order to scrutinize the private room, before the captain's return: De Barral has stolen into the room, his "short, puffy, old freckled hand" tremblingly swerving to the glass on the tray. Then he immediately withdraws to his own adjoining cabin, when the suspicious Powell suddenly comes down from the quarter-deck and opens the door to the saloon, with the sole aim "to remove the suspected tumbler." The suspense of this scene is electrifying in its urgency and incredulity, and is heightened by Captain Anthony's sudden reappearance, catching Powell in the act of running out with the glass of "brandy-and-water" in his hand. Powell, like a man in a trance, is arrested by "a voice asking him what he was doing there in tones of thunder." This is yet another superbly crafted episode in *Chance*, what with an ashamed and desperate Powell transfixed, as if in a dreamlike state, and Anthony staggered by what he beholds in front of him: his second officer, "a seemingly decent, well-bred young man," who had left his post and sneaked into the saloon "for the expressibly mean purpose of drinking up what was left of his captain's brandy-and-water."

A "monstrosity of appearances" shocks both the captain and the second mate, awonder, in an atmosphere of shudder and surprise. "The air was unbreathable, thick, sticky, odious, like hot jelly in which all movements became difficult." Language itself seems to tremble, as the words from Powell's lips come forth, mumbling and straining, the power of language itself overwhelmed, defied by the nature of the conditions and circumstances of their baffling encounter: "Doctored. . . . I believe," as he puts the glass down on the tray. Anthony moves to retrieve the glass, and, in turn, Powell, his legs shaking, his vision confused, his mind expectant, screams in a "strangled whisper," "Don't, sir! Don't touch it." "Who was it?" Captain Anthony asks, astonished by his subordinate's amazing revelation, as Powell himself goes on to recount for his captain the sequential gestures of an evil motion masking an equally evil intention.

In this dramatic scene Conrad is the supreme controlling master of language and context and insight. The appearance of Flora at this point reinforces "the tension to the breaking point." Both the captain and Powell try to protect her from knowing about the incident and strive to allay her concern. Simultaneously de Barral himself now also appears, causing a cold shudder to run down Powell's back: the father's blatant presence here, given the crisis of the past two hours, unnerves the young mate—"wonder, horror, indignation." The physical details of each of the four figures seen together here help to define a supremely "psychological moment": Flora, looking "like a forsaken elf"; Captain Anthony, with "something African, something Moorish" about him; de Barral, glancing "with a sort of underhand expectation at the captain and Mrs. Anthony standing close together"; Powell, "like a child, sensitive, impressionable, plastic." Somehow, too, we have a sense of Flora unconsciously drawn into a "close communion" with the captain, reigniting in her "the force of his personal fascination."

For Roderick Anthony, however, "the tension of the false situation was at its highest," as he finally recognizes the immensity of his plight, cogently identified in this narrative assessment: "And if two beings thrown together . . . fail in understanding and voluntarily stop short of the—the embrace, in the noblest meaning of the word, then they are committing a sin against life, the call of which is simple. Perhaps sacred." Feelings of desperation, the opposing and perplexing tugs of passion, the yearning for "the embrace" and also the resistance to it, possess Roderick at this most critical point of their relationship. Anthony, now being ruled by his sense of futility, comes to the unhappiest conclusion, as he says to Flora: "I am not blind. . . . I can't fight any longer for what I haven't got. . . . I give up. . . . You shall go," even as he overhears behind his back "a triumphant chuckling sound" coming from the old man. Anthony accepts the fact that de Barral has prevailed: "He shall have his way with you—and with me. . . . I shall let you go," he says, feverishly, to his wife.

For Flora, "stiffened into the very image of astonishment," Anthony's "incomprehensible words" incite a luminous moment of recantation and recognition, and she cries out, "But I don't want to be let off. . . . You can't cast me off like this, Roderick. I won't go away from you." Her words signal de Barral's defeat, as he puckers his eyes "at the sight of his daughter clinging around Captain Anthony's neck"—a sight that marks the moral victory of "the embrace" and the consummation of the love that has, for years, eluded the couple. The captain, "awakening to his opportunity . . . began to partly support her, partly carry her in the direction of her cabin." The climactic disappearance of Flora and Roderick Anthony in the stern-cabin is confluent with the removal from their lives of de Barral, who has in essence served as Conrad's agent of "spiritual obliteration."

To the end, de Barral refuses to accept the intrinsic goodness of the captain, "a man in a million," and further insists that his daughter has herself conspired against him, "till she has fairly put my head under the heel of that jailor, of that scoundrel, of her husband. . . . Treachery! Bringing me low." Clearly his titanic pride has been dealt a blow; he cannot believe that he has failed in his malevolent purpose. The idea that he has been defeated obsesses and finally defeats de Barral. In the presence of young Powell, then, and overpowered by his own evil, de Barral snatches the captain's glass, containing the same capsule of poison that his pitying physician had years before provided the great financier, and that he had kept on his person from the last day of the trial, tosses the liquor down his throat and collapses. Powell rushes forward to lift up the body: "But directly he raised his shoulders he knew that the man was dead! Dead!" Captain Anthony, hearing Powell's call for help, silently looks down at the dead body. They exchange stealthy glances without a word, and proceed to lift up the rigid body and to place it in a swinging cot. "The steward will find him in the morning," the captain declares to Powell. The captain and young Powell are sworn to "Silence for ever about this." And for near on six years following de Barral's turning "the abominable weapon against himself," Powell remained contentedly with Captain and Mrs. Anthony, sailing all over the world.

Powell, in supplying his factual recollection of his experiences on the ship to the anonymous first-person narrator and to Marlow, thus brings closure to the historical reconstruction of the fragments that make up Flora's life story. The *Ferndale*, we learn from Powell, who is no longer the young mate who had ten years earlier joined the crew of that ship, was lost at sea: "Sunk. Collision. And Captain Anthony went down with her." Four years after the fact, an inconsolable Powell describes the collision, which occurs during a "flat calm and a fog thick enough to slice with a knife," with a Belgian Green Star liner, the *Westland*. Anthony and Powell help to save Flora, and in turn Anthony helps to save Powell, the selfless captain being the last to leave the ship. "The *Ferndale* went down like a stone and Captain Anthony went down with her, the finest man's soul that ever left a sailor's body." It is Powell who relates to Flora, in the first-class saloon of the *Westland*, the fate of her husband. And before the week was out, it was Flora helping Powell to pull himself together. At this point of the narrative, we also learn from Powell's account that Mrs. Anthony, not much over thirty, is residing in a village in England. A retired, greying sailor, he is now a yachtsman who owns a little five-ton cutter that he sails alone, especially in the mouth of the creek. It is evident that Powell still visits Flora—that he is, in fact, courting her.

Through Powell's mediation, Marlow pays Flora a visit and finds her still "like a fine tranquil afternoon." She admits to writing the "foolish" letter to Mrs. Fyne, who once labeled her "a heartless adventuress" to her brother, that had "caused little Fyne to interfere in that offensive manner," explaining that she really thought that she was selling herself to Captain Anthony. Only later did she discover her love for Roderick, noting that her father's "prejudice against Roderick was her greatest grief." But in Captain Anthony, she also notes, she finally found a true and reciprocal love, kindness, safety, as well as the beauty and charm of sea-life. In these last few pages of *Chance* there is a wonderful, bracing flush of affirmation, of hope and happiness, of joy "beyond endurance, beyond desperation." Conrad's vision of human existence has mellowed, unafraid to see life in a mellifluous light, when, in Flora's own words, "The most familiar things appeared lighted up with a new light, clothed with a loveliness I had never suspected."

Perhaps it is this greater vision, precarious as it is, bravely accepting the moral possibility of renewal, that the critics who dismiss *Chance* are unprepared to accept, and who, in effect, admit to their own limitations and even to their cynicism about any possibility of moral ascent that transcends despair and horror. Conrad's vision of affirmation shimmers and glows here as we perceive how Powell himself has given up the sea in order to follow Flora and to relieve her aloneness, and to give to her the love that surpasses his love for the sea. It is especially interesting to see Marlow here joining Conrad in encouraging Flora to yield to the possibility of the love that Powell, as patient and selfless as his late captain, has been proffering to her since first boarding the *Ferndale*.

At the end of *Chance* Conrad leaves us with a benevolent vision of generosity and magnanimity, the enduring and blessed virtues that illumine the figures of Flora and Powell, standing silently together at the bank of the river, at high water, to hail Marlow as he sets sail, in the dusk. This luminous parting scene, confident and expectant, helps to reconfirm the aptness of Virginia Woolf's summary praise of *Chance* in her essay, "Mr. Conrad: A Conversation" (1923), which is written in the form of a dialogue between two "old friends," Penelope Otway and David Lowe, as they discourse on the subject, "Mr. Conrad is a classic," and that ends with these words: " 'I have just read *Chance*,' said Penelope. 'It is a great book, I think. But now you will have to read it yourself, for you are not going to accept my word, especially when it is a word which I cannot define. It is a great book, a great book,' she repeated."[7]

[7]*Collected Essays*, 1st American ed. (New York, 1967) 1:313.

Chapter 7

The Rover

First conceived as a short story, *The Rover* is Joseph Conrad's last complete novel. He finished the manuscript in July 1922 after eight months of steady writing. The novel itself was published on December 3, 1923, and quickly became a commercial and popular success. Not long after, on August 3, 1924, Conrad died suddenly of a heart attack at the age of sixty-seven. His death occurred at "Oswalds," the name of Conrad's last house, in Bishopsbourne, near Canterbury, Kent, where he had been living since 1919. Inscribed on Conrad's tombstone in Canterbury cemetery are two lines from Edmund Spenser's *The Faerie Queene*:

> Sleepe after toyle, port after stormie seas,
> Ease after warre, death after life, does greatly please.

These lines also serve as the epigraph to *The Rover*. Though in several of his letters Conrad was to express a dislike of "the Christian religion, its doctrines, ceremonies, and festivals,"[1] he was buried with the last rites of the Roman Catholic Church at St. Thomas's in Canterbury on August 7, 1924. Conrad's own words perhaps answer those who stress his "imaginative atheism." "Profanity is the preserve of the devil," we hear him saying. "Don't assume . . . that I do not believe, I do; all true seamen do in their hearts."

I

The Rover also completes the moral pattern of Conrad's vision as a novelist. In it the moral warfare that occupied so much of his attention in his major novels comes to its conclusion. Here Conrad reveals how moral conflict, with all of its jagged edges and jarring tensions, reaches a resolution that proclaims discovery in affirmation. In essence *The Rover* is his farewell, as well as his journey's end, lacking in this instance any need for still another familiar authorial note since it is a novel that conveys his last

---

[1]Letters to Edward Garnett, dated December 22, 1902, and February 23, 1914, in *Letters from Joseph Conrad, 1895–1924*, edited and with an introduction and notes by Edward Garnett (Indianapolis, c1928).

words and thoughts, his reaffirmation of his beliefs. Indeed, it is a novel that serves as a kind of epilogue; it simultaneously looks back on the past, as a historical chronicle, "[a] thing of sentiments—of many sentiments," as he specified in a letter. It is in effect about homecoming, going back to origins, reasserting one's essential self-in-connection. It is about the shock of recognition upon one's final return to Ithaca,[2] so to speak, or as Conrad wrote in a letter to John Galsworthy: "I have wanted for a long time to do a seaman's 'return' (before my own departure)."[3] Conrad was also clear about the technical aims of his valedictory novel of less than three-hundred printed pages. "This is perhaps my only work in which brevity was a conscious aim. I don't mean compression,"[4] he wrote.

The Rover relates the story, and the fate, of Master-Gunner Jean Peyrol who returns to his place of birth and early life in the Port of Toulon in southeastern France, located in the Peninsula of Giens, on the coast of the Mediterranean Sea, where Conrad himself had his earliest experiences of the sea. Dedicated, "In Friendship," to G. Jean-Aubry, Conrad adds the words, "This Tale of the Last Days of a French Brother of the Coast." Now, at that point in a life that had lasted for fifty-eight years, more than forty years spent as a buccaneer in the Indian Seas, "in lawless contests with his kind for a little loot that vanished as soon as grasped," Peyrol has returned as "a stranger to his native country." In the sunset years of his life, "tired of rolling about the seas," "he felt like a navigator about to land on a newly discovered shore." His return to Toulon, verily fusing mystery and poetry from the opening pages of the novel, is one of reverent expectation, longing as he does for "a period of repose."

All he now wants is a "quiet nook, an obscure corner out of men's sight where he could dig a hole unobserved." He arrives at approximately the beginning of the French Revolutionary Wars (1792–1800). Toulon is at this time safely in the hands of the revolutionaries who had, during the Siege of Toulon, August 27–December 19, 1793, occupied the city and its forts. It was during this battle, in fact, that a Jacobin Napoleon Bonaparte first distinguished himself as a young officer who helped take the city from French royalist and counterrevolutionary forces. Thus, in the opening pages of the

---

[2]See John Lehmann, *The Open Night* (New York, 1952) 58.

[3]Georges Jean-Aubry, *Joseph Conrad: Life and Letters*, vol. 2 (Garden City NY, 1927) 334.

[4]Garnett, 298.

novel, the old rover is called "Citoyen Peyrol," "a patriot and entitled to his discharge," who has now returned to a strangely familiar and unchanged geographical area of France, "in a landscape of stony hills, pale rocks, and dusty green of olive trees."

We learn that he has no notion at all of a father, even as he dimly remembered his mother, who had fallen ill and had died in the night. The place of his birth is also shrouded in mystery, though he has a vague idea that he had been born on the island of Porquerolles, just beyond the town of Hyères. The circumstances of his mother's death so terrified him that he ran off to a little place by the sea called Almanarre, where he hid in the hold of a tartane, lying there with no one on board. The crew of the tartane came on board some time during the night, and set sail for Marseilles. Discovered, he tried to explain to three bearded men that he had been working for a farmer named Peyrol, the name that henceforth stuck to him for life, since the boy of twelve did not know he had a name of his own. The memories of his native country stopped for him at this point of his life. We learn, too, that Peyrol's life at sea was to be one of great adventure on endless oceans—"of the Mozambique Channel, of Arabs and negroes, of Madagascar, of the coast of India, of islands and channels and reefs; of fights at sea, rows on shore, desperate slaughter and desperate thirst, of all sorts of ships one after another: merchant ships and frigates and privateers; of reckless men and enormous sprees."

A certain mystique surrounds his growing reputation as a Brother of the Coast. Inevitably, "new cries and new ideas" that accompanied the French political situation following the Revolution of 1789 came floating aboard ship from home, but these little affected "the slowly developed attention of the gunner Peyrol." These ideas were "the invention of landsmen," both removed from and antithetical to life at sea. Peyrol thus represents a non-political seaman, independent in his bearing and "magisterial" in his words, one who has in the course of his life and work not been involved in the wiles and struggles of men of the land. In this respect, Peyrol, "the man of violent deeds," comes across to us as singularly uncorrupted and guileless; a man who has necessarily cultivated the virtue of patience "that is so often a form of courage." The first three chapters of *The Rover* seek to establish Peyrol's character, etching out its peculiar qualities and temper, evoking his life-experiences, introducing his total persona to the reader, catching his uniqueness in a historical era of urgency, danger, fatefulness.

By bringing together the various fragments of Peyrol's life, in the context of time and space, and of past and present, Conrad enables the reader to comprehend the state of Peyrol's heart and soul, in preparation for a new life on land and the ensuing enactment of moral virtues that salvage the meaning of life from the terrors, treacheries, and tergiversations of "his revolutionized native land." Who is this homeless "sailor-man" who has now returned to live out the remainder of his life in a hamlet at the end of the Giens peninsula containing a few houses round a church and a farm? What role could he possibly play at "the end of the peninsula which . . . divides the picturesque roadstead of Hyères, from the headlands and curves of the coast forming the approaches of the Port of Toulon"? It is clear that Peyrol, "who had seen fights, massacres on land and sea, towns taken by assault by savage warriors, who had killed men in attack and defence," is at a different and final stage of his life when he arrives at Escampobar Farm. Here he will live in a tall farmhouse, in a large low room in the attic with its three windows having "a view of salt water on three sides." For Peyrol "It's like being in a lighthouse. . . . Not a bad place for a seaman to live in." And here, above the battle, as it were, Peyrol hopes to live "remote from all thoughts of strife and death, so full of smiling security, making all his past appear to him like a chain of lurid days and sultry nights."

Here, indeed, as an "inmate of Escampobar Farm," Peyrol's "instinct for rest had found its home at last." Seemingly, peace and security would be his to the end of his life; this "lighthouse" would be a sanctuary from which he could continuously view the world around him—"the immobility of a smiling enchantment, of a Mediterranean fair day, breathless sometimes but never without life." In one sense, Peyrol, as we see him at the beginning of the novel, has embarked on a paradisal quest that would give him rest from the toils of the sea, that would allow him to remain loyal to his memories of the past but also give him time for reflection, and that would help him transcend the monstrous world of the France of Marat, Robespierre, and Danton, "the able artificers in the trade and mystery of murder," to recall Edmund Burke's words. How, moreover, does one finally face the reality of death, and how does one do so, beyond despair, with the kind of moral fortitude that has characterized one's life as a sea rover? These are important questions that Peyrol will have to answer in his last years. At the same time, how does one preserve the Conradian principles of brotherhood and solidarity that are opposed to ideological systems, to political partisanship, and "the pettiness of national hatreds"?

Rightly, Conrad's biographer Frederick Karl describes *The Rover* as "a statement of values"[5]—of axiomatic moral values to be more precise. Conrad pays tribute to these values as they exemplify Peyrol's life, consistently and steadfastly. Peyrol, in this respect, is not only a man of action but also a conservator of values. Conrad does not in any way overdramatize Peyrol's achievement and meaning, and if anything his presence in the book is understated, with the stress on subtlety and nuance, rather than on demonstrative portrayal. His character is quietly heroic, without fanfare, manifesting reserve and reticence in depth and plenitude, always in sharp contrast to the beautiful and declamatory behavior and attitudes of "the shore breed." When asked upon his return to Toulon from whence he has come, his reply is revealing: "From the other side of the world." People's stares and whispers neither disturb nor distract him. For over four decades Peyrol has "knocked about the Eastern Seas," and has now returned to a land obsessed with the abstract ideals of liberty, equality, fraternity. At a time of discord and suspicion, Peyrol attests to a sense of honesty and directness: "As he went along the streets he looked as usual everybody in the eye. . . . It wasn't that he was afraid of anything. His mind was as calm as the natural set of his florid face."

Gravity and grace are qualities that he imparts, but there is nothing simplistic about him as we gradually learn from more details about his life. Mutiny; "crazy love for a yellow girl"; treachery; betrayal, the bizarre and the atrocious; "the panic of the supernatural" that touched him when his mother died "under a heap of rags"; and "another kind of terror" he felt on the quays of Marseilles, when he had been discovered hiding in the tartane, an almost fatal wound suffered blamelessly in a quarrel and a painful convalescence: these "graduations of experience" had taught him much. "No doubt all this was enough to make one die of fright, but that possibility never occurred to him." Fearlessness born of courage and discipline was his mainstay. "The necessities of a lawless life had taught Peyrol to be ruthless, but he had never been cruel."

It is worth recalling that when we first meet Peyrol his movements are slow and heavy because of the fact he wore next to his bare skin, "like a pious penitent his hair-shirt," a canvas waistcoat within which he hid a large treasure of foreign coins—gold mohurs, Dutch ducats, Spanish pieces, English guineas—equal to sixty or seventy thousand francs: "Loot big or

---

[5] *Joseph Conrad: The Three Lives* (New York, 1979) 865.

little was a natural freebooter's life"—and he was not going to give it up to anyone, whether to scheming members of his crew, or to greedy political authorities in Toulon, "confounded landsmen, mere sharks." His secret garment "tried his endurance" and restrained him from getting into trouble—"keep clear of rows, of intimacies, of promiscuous jollities." (He is even taken for a priest by a boatman he meets and who will show him the way to the inn at Escampobar Farm.) The waistcoat is still another sobering reason for Peyrol to be solitary and prudent, to see others through cautious eyes and to measure his speech. He entertains neither illusions nor unreal expectations in his view of people; his qualities of character thus arm him fully to live in a world that can suddenly and inexplicably turn on one. And one always had to be prepared, when confronting the world, never to underestimate its fury or to be lulled by its beauty. For Conrad, the character of Peyrol holds both practical and redeeming paradigms that enable one to be true to one's indwelling standards of discernment—balance, moderation, sincerity, but also firmness, probity, prudence.

Peyrol opposes abstract theories that culminate in ideology and the deformations of commonwealth and soul that inevitably accompany armed doctrines. Invariably Conrad's visionary social-political insights empower *The Rover*. Yet this is far more than a political or historical novel, even though politics and history are its constituent ingredients. Moral warfare and moral character circumscribe *The Rover*, and are what give to it meaning and define its transcendent moral message. Structurally, thematically, and integrally this novel can advantageously be approached in the context of Edmund Burke's belief that "In all moral machinery, the moral results are its test." For whatever happens in Peyrol's life-story has not only moral implications but also moral consequences. Peyrol mirrors the Conradian hero in form and practice, even as he personifies the legacy of Conrad's fundamental moral preoccupations. In Peyrol, Conrad is repeating and refining his conception of moral values in its enduring essences, beyond the historical moment or fleeting event. In a distinct sense, Peyrol and he speak to the human condition directly in its beginnings and endings, within and beyond historical boundaries.

In its immediate political ambience, *The Rover* seeks to contrast the morally redemptive values, which impel Peyrol, and those of a revolutionary France: the rejection of all moral order and the destruction of all humane norms through Regicide, Jacobinism, Atheism. Conrad makes unmistakably clear from the start just how dangerous are the conditions of the moral warfare that Peyrol enters when he returns to land. Here he beholds the hideous face of the enemy in the person of Citizen Scevola Bron, the "sansculotte" (derived from the word for long trousers worn by many of the French revolutionaries) who epitomizes the radical spirit of the Revolution and the rabble, the robbers and the murderers who implemented the Reign of Terror with unparalleled malignity and wickedness. Conrad's depiction of Scevola is pitilessly graphic from the first moment Peyrol encounters him at the inn on the outskirts of the town of Hyères. Scevola is the husband of Arlette, the young hereditary mistress of the inn; the picture of him that we derive from the text is emphatically odious and obscene. He is well known to the people of Toulon as one who "first became busy purveying the guillotine when they were purifying the town from all aristocrats." He belongs to the "drinkers of blood," "one of the best of them," indiscriminately killing "traitors in the streets, in cellars, in their beds." Peyrol actually meets Scevola, the master of the Escampobar Farm, only after briefly meeting his wife. An "ardent patriot," and "an object of fear and dislike," he was no more than thirty years old, "a well-made man of medium height, with a lack of resolution in his bearing." For him, even "Pity may be a crime."

In his depiction of Scevola, Conrad shows his known distaste for social breakdown and disorder, and he spares no detail in disclosing what the sansculotte represents and the dangers he poses for human order. Scevola is, then, still another of Conrad's "emissaries of death" seen in a pathologically political context. As a full-fledged agent of terror, he pursues "anti-revolutionary traitors" wherever they exist, and seeks to annihilate all "aristos." Indeed, in the most lurid crime of all, Citizen Scevola appears before a revolutionary tribunal to condemn Arlette's father and mother for collaborating with English seamen who had landed in Toulon, "in that cove at night and walk up to this very house." From this "dark story" we learn that Arlette's parents were actually executed in Toulon, after having been captured by the revolutionaries when they had come to take home their young daughter who had been living "with some skulking nuns." It is Scevola, her "patron," who brings back Arlette (whom he later marries) to the farm: " 'No lessons of base superstition could corrupt her soul,' he declared with exaltation. 'I brought home a patriot.' " Scevola's influence over the impressionable Arlette is insidious, as we come to find out, and as Peyrol himself discovers when he comes to the inn in search of lodgings.

Outwardly, at least, Arlette seems indoctrinated by Scevola: a revolutionary citoyenne, distrustful, distant, uneasy, somber, troubled in her bearing and speech when she first encounters Peyrol. She, too, like her mentor, Scevola, is in the grip of ideology. When she asks Peyrol, "Have you ever carried a woman's head on a pike?," he is bereft of speech. Peyrol is particularly struck by "The pure complexion of her white cheeks . . . set off brilliantly by her coral lips and the bands of raven-black hair. . . . " To him she is "like a sea-bird—not to be grasped." He becomes even more perplexed when "this strange creature dropped her eyelids, advanced quite close to him and began to finger the lapel of his coat—something that a child might have done." It is perhaps the rape of innocence that Peyrol, "touched by a soft indefinite emotion," intuits during his meeting with Arlette, who finally answers his request to stay at the farm (even "for ever") with these ominous words: "Yes. You may stay. I think we shall be friends. I'll tell you about the Revolution."

The Escampobar farmhouse becomes for Peyrol his last stop, this in spite of its cruel history and deviant occupants. At the end of the third chapter we have a serene picture of Peyrol in the "garret full of light" as he opens and examines "his big sandalwood chest." He had carried this chest with him in all sorts of places, leaving it behind for safe-keeping on the Madagascar coast, or with native chiefs, with Arabs, with friends, even with his enemies, and then losing and rediscovering it again "in Port Louis, of all places in the world, in a little dark den of a shop kept by a lone Hindoo." And, after all, was he not an old seaman who had learned not to become "surprised at anything that sea or land" can produce? Thus, having repacked his chest, Peyrol, "robust and grey-haired, his head with a Roman profile," is the picture of a man who is at peace with himself and with the world, and who is also beyond its afflictions and enmities: "Then he rose, and looking round the room and stretching his powerful arms, he ceased to think of the treasure, of the future and even of to-morrow, in the sudden conviction that he could make himself very comfortable there."

The Peyrol we first meet in *The Rover* sums up the heroic virtues that save one from joining the ranks of the mediocre and the tawdry. He has a long and close identity with the sea and clearly perceives his distinct differences with the land-world, its cruelties and machinations, epitomized by political revolution and social turmoil. He is a man of passion and instinct, whose heart is large and whose mind is circumspect but undefiled. His life at sea has necessarily taught him to survive by every possible means the dangers of the physical world. But mere survival is not the end-all for Peyrol insofar as he acquits himself with a quiet dignity and honesty uncompromised by expediency or meanness. He has about him an openness and a prescient intelligence (of character) that enable him to deal even with others who lack his qualities. As such, Peyrol intuitively recognizes the spirit of enmity, accepts its reality, but never knowingly embraces or abets it.

Some critics dismiss *The Rover* as "fag-end adventure-stuff,"[6] or as a "sentimental and flabbily romantic"[7] work. Regrettably their critiques confuse Conrad's language of openness and his beneficent vision with what they call his "essentially meaningless rhetoric."[8] Conrad's story of Peyrol's return captures the moral undercurrents of a world in the throes of devolution. Peyrol is Conrad's prism of clarity through which we gauge the full extent of the modern world's worship of strange gods and of its confusion of values and its oppressiveness. The world to which Peyrol returns is a fallen world that refuses, in the end, to give him the rest he yearns for, and will in fact strive to make him still another slave of slaves. Peyrol thus returns to be thrown in the vortex of a world in disarray, of which revolutionary France is the epicenter. The early chapters of *The Rover* render precisely the dynamics of such a world, into which Peyrol is drawn and which he will struggle to understand and to resist its abominations. His moral impulses face their greatest test in how he meets a new-old world, and how he preserves the strengths of character that distinguish him from a Scevola, the sansculotte, "a creature of the universal blood-lust of the time," thirsting endlessly for savage deeds and murder.

To be sure, Peyrol has lived most of his life away from civilized society, and his return to it progressively exposes the malevolence that lies just beneath the surface, ready to strike out with vengeance. It is to such a world that an essentially innocent Peyrol returns and which he finally chooses to oppose, if he is not to be devoured by its might. As an "old skimmer of the seas," Peyrol has suffered ordeals of great magnitude; he has wrestled with adversity unto death itself again and again. But now, settled on the peninsula of France, Peyrol must face radical conditions and circumstances: "The Revolution had made a clean cut across the consistency of his wild life—Brother of the Coast and gunner in the national navy—and yet he was the same man." It is made abundantly evident that Peyrol's return to France is

---

[6]*Conrad: A Collection of Critical Essays*, ed. Marvin Mudrick (Englewood Cliffs NJ, 1966) 10.

[7]Martin Tucker, *Joseph Conrad* (New York, 1976) 100.

[8]Thomas Moser, *Joseph Conrad: Achievement and Decline* (Cambridge MA, 1957) 177ff.

also his introduction to a modern social order in which the verities of loyalty, trust, magnanimity are discarded and sacrificed on the altar of betrayal.

II

Peyrol's loyalty to the old verities is the sequential subject of the remaining sixteen chapters of *The Rover*. These chapters illuminate the complex fate of "the man of dark deeds, but of large heart." Eight years have now passed since the Siege of Toulon in 1793, ending with the proclamation of Napoleon as Consul for life, 1802-. Peyrol, "sea-rover turned rustic," is past his mid-sixties, "his strong thick head of hair . . . nearly all white now." He is addressed as "Monsieur Peyrol." This marks the time of the British fleet's blockade, under the command of Lord Nelson, of the harbor of Toulon in 1803. The Peyrol we see here is the man who proves himself to be a true patriot, unbought and unsold. He is sharply contrasted with Scevola ("A Jacobin, if ever there was one."); Conrad fastidiously seeks to show how antipodal their value-systems are. In particular the moral character of each man is delineated as the reader is made aware of their deeds and mind-set.

Scevola, a born sansculotte, with "a red cap on his head," is unswerving in his Jacobin faith. In him, revolutionary ideology in the form of anti-Christian animosity has caught a strangle hold: "[t]he church bell is like poison to him." If other sansculottes managed to soften their animus, Scevola remains adamant in his views; there is something flat and grotesque about him that in the end reveals him as an ideological epigone, a mediocre functionary who lives purely for his malevolence. Peyrol's incisive words go to the core of Scevola's miscreant character: "This one won't change his skin, and as to his inside he never had anything in him that could be moved." The more the reader sees and hears of Scevola, the more does the reader appreciate, by juxtaposition, Peyrol's inherent moral strengths. For what we see in explicit ways is Peyrol's gradual emergence from a paradisal refuge (even illusion) to his assuming responsibilities as an *engagé* human being, his willingness to take a principled stand and, in short, to commit himself to the requisites of moral action. Indeed, we can measure Peyrol's development in terms of Scevola's immersion in his baseness: "By himself he was nothing. He had never been anything but a creature of the universal blood-lust of the time."

Those whose lives Peyrol touches are literally saved; he is a well of beneficences, in whose presence men and women, who are seemingly lost or morally atrophied, are awakened to their better selves. Lieutenant Eugène Réal and Arlette exemplify Peyrol's beneficent powers to transform lives. Réal is a young naval officer who encounters Peyrol unexpectedly settled in the peninsula. Réal is an "orphan of the Revolution": after eight years of service on the ships of the Republic, he has "arrived at the rank of an officer by sheer merit." A detached, "self-contained" man, like Peyrol himself, he had adopted at sea "another standard of values." His principles, we learn, were purely professional and he had "never formed a friendship in his life." Peyrol is "the first human being to break through the schooled reserve" of the young officer. He arouses the interest of Réal, who feels "a mistrustful liking with some contempt of a doctrinaire kind" with respect to Peyrol's past—"a sort of past which could not commend itself to a naval officer." But what also most impresses Réal is Peyrol's "faculty of shrewd insight." His meeting with Peyrol occurs in the course of Réal's doing shore duty in Toulon, and spending periods of short leave (or possibly duty) at the farm. A sort of father-son friendship between the two men evolves, with the profoundest consequences for both.

The actual reasons for Réal's visits to the farm are somewhat vague: "He had been growing sick of his work. He had no place in the world to go to, and no one either. Was it Peyrol he was coming to see?" In any case, a "mute, strangely suspicious, defiant understanding" eventually established itself during a period of two years between the young officer who is obviously at loose ends at this point in his life, and the "lawless old man," who seemed to have come to the Escampobar Farm simply to die. Thus their coming together, in rather strange circumstances and conditions, occurs at a time when each man senses a life-emptiness, a purposelessness, in existence. Indeed, their strange meeting is salvific for it enables them to join in a common cause when together they cautiously observe the movements of an "enemy ship" nearby, the twenty-two gun English sloop *Amelia*, which has for nearly a year acted as "the extreme lookout ship of Admiral Nelson's blockading fleet," and which has "drifted so far within Cape Esterel that the low projecting mass of it seemed to be in actual contact with her stern."

Captain Vincent, who commands the *Amelia*, has ordered a "nocturnal expedition" to the area of the peninsula in which the farm is located. The secret landing is to be led by Mr. Bolt, a master's mate, who knew a great deal about the Escampobar Farm at the entrance of the Toulon harbor ever since many years ago he had repeatedly visited the farmhouse while serving in Lord Howe's fleet. It was Bolt who had first told Captain Vincent about the farm's early royalist connections and aroused the latter's curiosity as to its strategic importance to the English in the present blockade. Captain Vincent then dispatches Bolt to land a boat on the beach near the farm, monitor the situation carefully, and gather whatever information he could, and, from time to time, "go down in the dead of night, signal to the ship and make his report," serving in effect as "The actual eyes of Lord Nelson's fleet! Not long after, however, Mr. Bolt returns to the *Amelia* to tell the captain that his mission has been a "dismal failure," also mumbling, "There are night-walkers there." Clearly, for Bolt, "there had been changes in that farmhouse since his time." It had now taken on "the aspect of a man trap"; and its "fascination of repose, of secretive friendliness . . . was gone." Bolt, hence, had come "quickly to the conclusion that he must withdraw from the slope." Bolt also hastens to blurt out that "he had lost a man" from the boat's crew of five members: "It was as if Symons had been spirited away by some supernatural means, without a scuffle, without a cry."

Actually, as it turns out, Symons, the lost English seaman, and formerly, like Peyrol, a Brother of the Coast, had been discovered by Peyrol, who with his "trusty cudgel" knocked Symons over with a blow at the back of the head. This event occurred one night on the hillside when Peyrol had come to sleep in his tartane and had espied Symons ("Landed from an English boat.") looking down suspiciously at the vessel: "The force of the blow flung the senseless body over the edge of the flat rock and down headlong into the open hold of the tartane, which received it with the sound of a muffled drum." Some years past Peyrol had found and renovated an abandoned two-masted tartane and kept it moored in the cove below the Escampobar Farm. Michel, the fisherman of the lagoon, was enlisted for the "crew" and lived on board the tartane docked in the concealed basin. ("He was the last of men. Somebody must be last. There was no place for him in the life of the village.") The only company Peyrol had in the course of laboriously repairing the vessel ("a dreadful mess") was "a hunchbacked cripple" who lived in the hamlet; originally the tartane belonged to the Escampobar and "had taken Arlette's parents to their death in the vengeful massacre of Toulon" and "had brought back the youthful Arlette and Citizen Scevola" to the farm.

In the cripple Peyrol discerns qualities that, in Conrad's novels, define character and strength—"there was manliness in that twisted scrap of humanity which struck Peyrol from the first." In particular the cripple helps clarify for Peyrol some of the brutal conditions found in the years of the Revolution. In his various, if necessarily limited, ways the cripple helps Peyrol to complete successfully the renovation of the tartane, and embodies for the rover (and for Conrad) traits that best define character, fidelity. Peyrol pays him the highest compliment: " 'I tell you,' insisted the rover roughly, and as if the insignificance of mortal envelopes had presented itself to him for the first time at the end of his roving life, 'I tell you that there is that in you which would make a chum one would like to have alongside one in a tight place.' " Within the total economy of *The Rover*, it will be thus seen, Conrad invariably weaves into his text the values that are morally redeeming in the human world.

Peyrol's treatment of the battered Symons testifies to his code of ethics in practice. Peyrol's expression of concern for Symons's life is seen as genuine, as his listless body is carefully lowered into the tartane's cabin. There is, in fact, a certain tenderness in Peyrol's attention to another, and in this case an English seaman's fate: "The dripping head with soaked hair was like the head of a drowned man with a gaping pink gash on the forehead." There is no trace of animosity or vengefulness or triumphalism in Peyrol's conduct as he attends to the body. Even when Symons wakes to consciousness, now fully aware of his plight, and "swearing feebly without intermission," Peyrol is patient and considerate in his responses, accepting his responsibility for Symons's injury, at the same time honestly giving his reasons for the blow to the head: "Because you put your nose where you [had] no business. Understand?" Even when Symons attacks Peyrol for "play[ing] a damned dirty trick on me," the Rover remains steady and calm, feeling no repulsion as he confronts a Brother who "turned into this English man-of-war's man."

Peyrol's devotion to duty, as it were, is also rooted in a humaneness that is never compromised. (After all, "mutual protection was the first duty between Brothers of the Coast.") And, as Conrad reminds us, Peyrol's conduct must be observed evaluatively against the backdrop of the Revolution's fanatical ideology—its "cold malignity of a wicked spirit," to use Edmund Burke's words. In distinct and forceful ways, Peyrol is Conrad's rejoinder to "the antagonist world" that destroys virtues of magnanimity and benevolence and that demeans and oppresses the individual human personality in its obsessive pursuit of power. Peyrol is Conrad's reiteration of those heroic qualities that a humane civilization, if it is to survive, must strive to preserve and to revere. Conrad's "conscious aim" in *The Rover*, to achieve "brevity" as opposed to "compression," can be better understood in terms of the major creedal principles he renders in this novel, especially in the person of Peyrol, who ("so different from all mankind") embodies precisely the "standard of values" that the lieutenant acquired at sea. Peyrol transmits this standard to the land-world: to assert its living principle as a universal brotherhood. Scenes of revolution and destruction recur in *The Rover*, whether as direct events or as narrated flashbacks. This is Conrad's way of reminding the reader of the devastating power of "the terrors of a Judgment Day in which the world had been given over to the devils."

Arlette's anguished recollections of terror have a dramatic impact as she recalls the time she was being brought up in a convent in Toulon, "trapped in that town of tumult and confusion. . . . Appalling explosions of gunpowder shook the earth," as "dreadful men and many fierce women . . . ran along the streets brandishing pikes and sabres, pursuing other groups of unarmed people, who fled round corners with loud shrieks." Conrad is undaunted in portraying anarchism in the form of "Satan taking possession of rebellious mankind, exposing the nakedness of hearts like flint and of the homicidal souls of the Revolution." Yet no scene in the novel is more alleviating than when a penitential Arlette determinedly makes her way to a church near Escampobar: "But what drew her on was the church-tower, where, in a round arch, she could see the black speck of the bell which escaping the requisitions of the Republican wars, and dwelling mute above the locked-up empty church, had only lately recovered its voice." The picture of Arlette, kneeling on the steps before the great altar, her face "buried in her hands in a passion of piety and prayer," underlines those feelings of reverence that Conrad repeatedly expresses in his novels.

Arlette's metamorphosis from a wild and confused state of mind owes much to Peyrol's presence in the farmhouse. "Peyrol was the first human being she had noticed for years. Peyrol, since he had come, had always existed for her." In a sense, Arlette is reborn at this time, now that she has finally transcended the virus of the Revolution; not only is she now "new to life" but also to love, as she slowly realizes her powerful love for the lieutenant, her "delight to be near him, to watch him covertly, to hear him perhaps utter a few words, to experience that strange satisfying consciousness of her own existence which nothing but Réal's presence could give her." Their growing love, presided over by Peyrol, is calmly and tenderly, even playfully, presented, anchored in the Conradian qualities of "warmth, courage, confidence." Before Peyrol's arrival, Arlette is silent, suspicious, sullen. "You reward the child wonderfully," Catherine, Arlette's aged aunt, and the sister of the girl's father, says to Peyrol. It is as if "Papa Peyrol" has the miraculous power to transform others who live in darkness; he instinctively conveys life-giving and life-honoring principles of belief, and is a stranger to the denial of the meaning of life, "this intimate inward sense of the vanity of all things, that doubt of the power within himself."

But danger is never far off even in the most ardent experiences of love; there is always the possibility of a "treacherous blow" befalling the relationship between the two: "The lieutenant is the child of some ci-devant and Arlette of a man they called a traitor to his country." In this case, the real threat is posed by Scevola, who stands for anti-life; he is the shadow that falls between appearance and reality. It is he, in fact, who presents the most immediate danger to the lieutenant, since Scevola wants to deprive him of "his right to Arlette": "He became giddy with virtuous fury. There was enough evidence there for any revolutionary tribunal to cut all their heads off." Scevola embodies for Conrad an agent of evil, "greedily" armed with a stable fork, awaiting to pounce upon Réal upon his return from Toulon. In him we view the demonic energy run riot, as he "glares" at things around him, his teeth chattering with "savage impatience," his body "visible in his death-like rigidity," "an apparition not belonging to this earth." Scevola is still another of Conrad's devils who has "the fixed idea" "to get at the lieutenant unawares, and if the fellow died without knowing what hand had struck him, so much the better."

That, too, Conrad invests Scevola with an acutely ideological dimension extends and intensifies his demonic deformation so that in him habitual propulsion to things evil is further sharpened by his political corruption. His is, as such, a moral sliminess menacing community and soul; his evil outreach honors no bounds and inevitably affects the whole gamut of civilized existence, institutions as well as human beings. He lashes out indiscriminately in his acts of atrocity for the sake of atrocity; nothing and no one remains safe from his distorted loyalties: "The motive force of a fixed idea is very great." The implosive characteristic of the evil he is and the evil he does captures the full range of his nature, on extraphysical and extratemporal levels of operation. Physically Scevola is not at all imposing, "like a sparrow in body." Mentally he is mediocre in his language and thought, which makes him all the more intimidating, as he spouts clichés. A certain inconsequentiality hovers about him, once his Revolutionary creed has been exposed for what it is, morally vacuous. He does not have to think about the consequences of the doctrine he mouths or the terrors he commits as a slave of ideology.

When Scevola declares that "What has lost us was moderation," he reveals the basic thinking of the "blind and bloody band of sansculottes," as Burke expresses it. Scevola is an offshoot of the "Society of the Jacobins, Friends of Liberty and Equality," the political group that was prominent during the French Revolution, in the years 1789–1792, and that, as "centers of virtue," sought to protect what the Revolution had accomplished against any revival of aristocracy. The "spirit of Jacobinism," allied as it was with "the destructive wrath of Sansculottism," was to fill "France with hatreds, suspicions, scaffolds, and Reason-worship."[9] One of the important aims of the sansculottes, as agents of terror supported in turn by the Jacobins as agents of the revolutionary government, was to do away with any traces of moderation in France's political thought and activity. This Jacobin and sansculotte connection can be easily identified in Scevola's attitude and behavior. "We patriots held our hand too soon," he insists. "All the children of the ci-devants and all the children of traitors should have been killed together with their fathers and mothers. Contempt for civic virtues and love of tyranny were inborn in them all. They grow up and trample on all the sacred principles. . . . "

Scevola's hate for the lieutenant leads him to the tartane, where he believes the naval officer is hiding. At the sight of Scevola, Symons, who has now managed to drag himself out of the cabin and to hide at the fore-end of the tartane, was to break into perspiration; this "excellent able seaman of proved courage" is terrified at the sight of Scevola, "weird and dangerous in the extreme," manifesting a "homicidal purpose." Scevola, who has concluded that the lieutenant was out of the tartane, goes down to the cabin so as to discover "anything compromising," which instances a "Soldier of the Republic," answering to the Revolutionary order, "Do thy duty, *Fais ton devoir*." This gives Symons the chance to leave his concealed position, and to fling himself "on the doors of the cabin which came together with a crash." With Scevola locked in the cabin, Symons decides to scramble ashore, with the hope that somehow he would be able to reach at last the safety of the *Amelia* lying nearby. On higher ground, Peyrol detects the descending movements of his former prisoner and "his once useful chum," as he also sees a boat and then another boat from the ship gliding into view: "Peyrol's alarm for his tartane grew intolerable."

---

[9]See Thomas Carlyle, *The French Revolution: A History* (New York, 1934) 659.

The upshot of this episode is that Symons is rescued, as Peyrol himself hurries back at midnight to the farmhouse where he is to meet Lieutenant Réal on his return from Toulon. This entire episode (in chapter 13) again exemplifies Conrad's imaginative powers in creating suspense, a pendulous state of uncertainty and expectation, to be masterfully resolved in the climactic scenes described in the last three chapters (14, 15, 16) of *The Rover*, and that constitute, as John Lehmann believes, "a great poetic tragedy."[10] The tragedic dimension intensifies the final movement of *The Rover* as people and places, and historical actions and events, come to a culmination in the triumph of love and of death as heroic sacrifice. The novel thus concludes on a heightened note of release and salvation, at an intrinsically spiritual level. Here we see Peyrol as the redeemer of Réal and Arlette. He saves Réal from the demons of self-doubt, from the boredom and misanthropy that nullify "all capacity for the softer emotions": "Taciturn and guarded, he had formed no intimacies. Relations he had none. He had kept clear of social connections." Réal's nonlife brings to mind the deep passional concerns in novels by D. H. Lawrence and E. M. Forster in the early decades of the twentieth century and also echoes the disenchantment of the 1914–1918 war years. The "clamouring falsehoods of revolution," and the bleak ideology that accompanied it, hurled him into a state of anger, suspicion, fatigue, and left him a victim of life-emptiness entertaining even the thought of suicide. His continuous movements between Toulon and the farmhouse accentuate his feelings of self-division. He becomes the epitome of modern man in search of a soul.

Réal's emerging relationship with Peyrol alerts him to qualities of character that are restorative. Thus, when the lieutenant and Peyrol reunite just after the latter has made his way to the farm, following Symons's escape to the safety of the *Amelia*, both experience a feeling of relief: "The moon, the only witness of the meeting, seemed to shine on two friends so identical in thought and feeling that they could commune with each other without words." For Réal, "old Peyrol" conveys strength, confidence, self-control; also mystery and fable; and sincerity: "the only man who had nothing to do with the revolution—who had not even seen it at work. . . . That one was neither a hypocrite or a fool. When he robbed or killed it was not in the name of the sacred revolutionary principles or for the love of humanity." In *The Rover* the reader, no less than the lieutenant, comes to perceive

---

[10]Lehmann, 62.

Peyrol's character slowly and subtly as the gunner's past deeds and present circumstances converge to reveal him to be one who transcends ignoble human motives, wiles, meretriciousness, tendentiousness.

Peyrol's character and presence in the novel underline the authenticity of a life instinctively responsive to uncloyed and unclogged values. He is, in essence, a man of action, neither saint nor sage; a survivor who has navigated dangerous shoals and who has struggled with adversity, who has above all accepted reality with courage and without illusions: with "the sincere lawlessness of the ex-Brother of the Coast." If his sundry exploits seem to be clouded in romance, he is hardly a romanticist. He has seen and experienced too much to be beguiled by tales of chivalry or dreams of utopia. Neither metaphysical nor abstract theories can deter him from a keen awareness of the world as it is and in which one must live and struggle. As such, his moral dynamic, cumulatively tested, tried, and shaped in the process of a long and active life, conveys robustness and vitality. In this respect, as it has been suggested, Peyrol brings to mind Homer's Odysseus ("the man of many turns").[11] Not unlike Odysseus, Peyrol ("the man of dark deeds but of large heart") seeks in the end to alleviate the sufferings of men and women and to effect a climate of generosity and concord within the realm of human limitations. Ultimately what Réal sees in Peyrol, or at best intuits, is a man worthy of praise.

III

Peyrol's strength of character graces the concluding chapters of *The Rover*. The full value of his legacy is essentialized here in its moral ramifications, and in the reiterated context of Conrad's affirmation of solidarity and brotherhood. In a sense, Peyrol speaks Conrad's last words to the reader, and bridges both theory and practice in rendering his fundamental beliefs directly, memorably. We have in Peyrol, then, Conrad's testament of faith in all of its distinguishing accents and tones. What, exactly, shows Peyrol's special worthiness? Why does Peyrol deserve one's gratitude? Why should Peyrol be remembered? What, exactly, validates the stated claim that "the recollection of his white-headed, quiet, irresistible personality haunted every corner of the Escampobar fields"? In some ways, of course, these are perplexing questions that have long perplexed Conrad's critics, and no

[11]Ibid., 58.

doubt Conrad himself, insofar as he was investing Peyrol with qualities that exemplify moral heroism. Unfortunately, Conrad did not, in the case of *The Rover*, append an author's note (of explanation) as he often did in his major novels. And that is why, too, the final movement of this novel needs to be weighed so as to determine its right to distinction as that valedictory "statement about values" with which *The Rover* is identified.

The proof of the highmindedness, or "greatsouledness" in an Aristotelian sense, that attests to Peyrol's character, and to the moral excellences that Conrad assigns to him, and by which he wants him to be remembered, interlaces the final fateful episode of the novel. The episode ("Not an operation of war, but service of the greatest importance") has to do with a scheme "to deceive the English Admiral," the order itself coming from Bonaparte. Lieutenant Réal has been assigned the task of compiling a packet of faked dispatches and letters "containing a clear statement besides hints calculated to convince the enemy that the destination of the fleet now fitting in Toulon is for Egypt and generally for the East." More specifically, it will be Réal's responsibility to send the packet "by sea in some small craft to Naples, taking care that the vessel shall fall into the enemy's hands." The lieutenant chooses to get the help of Peyrol, whom he considers a patriotic Frenchman. They could make use of the *Amelia* in capturing an old vessel by the fleet in ways that would not arouse suspicion by the English interceptors. Both understand the dangers of the planned deception. It will be Peyrol's "moral obligation," as Réal expresses it, to let the lieutenant have the gunner's renovated tartane, on which the secret packet of false documents will be placed.

As the plan to trick the English proceeds, so too does the love relationship between Réal and Arlette accelerate in passion and scope. Every principle of honour and decency, as he said to himself, forbade him from trifling with the girl's feelings, but the unleashed power of eros had progressively overwhelmed him, making him its prisoner: "And then it suddenly dawned on him that he had been thinking of nothing but that woman for days. . . . mastered by an unworthy passion for a mere envelope, stained with crime and without a mind." "But whenever Arlette crossed his line of sight it was as if something had moved in his breast." "All in her is mystery, seduction, enchantment." "He flung his arms around her waist and hugged her close to his breast." Réal finds that, in the end, he cannot keep away from Escampobar, from Arlette, even as he is "on a service for which he had volunteered." To be sure, Réal knows he has his "duty" to fulfill ("tomorrow morning," in fact), even if it means death. The pull of eros and the thought of possible death are at war in Réal's heart, as he begins to question severely not only his patriotic duty but also his personal courage. Conrad renders Réal's inner conflict with extraordinary and undiminishing power of insight into passion and empathy for suffering: "Natures schooled into insensibility when once overcome by a mastering passion are like vanquished giants ready for despair. He, a man on service, felt himself shrinking from death and that doubt contained in itself all possible doubts of his own fortitude." Clearly, the unfolding dramatic intensity of this part of *The Rover*, no less than Conrad's profound control of craft, belies the charge that this novel discloses "the exhaustion of creative energy."[12] Conrad is as fully engaged in *The Rover* as he is in his major achievements.

When the day comes for the tartane to set sail in its mission of deception, Réal's appearance shows much tension: "Here is one who looks like a moth scorched in a fire." Fatality is in the air on the morning Réal makes his way to the basin of the cave where the tartane is harbored. Soon after a pensive and troubled Peyrol also finds his way to the tartane, perceiving the figures of Réal and Michel on board, as well as Citizen Scevola, who is tied up to a stanchion. "The great moment," for Réal, is approaching, though he is heavy-hearted and remorseful as he thinks of the prospects of his task. The darkening atmosphere, silent and shadowy, is now more ominous with "a sort of flicker of sunshine succeeded by a mighty but distant clap of thunder," as "a mysterious change seemed to come over the quality and colour of the light." Simultaneously, Arlette, in the farmhouse, has awakened from "an awful dream" in which she has seen Réal being attacked by a mob, "all dripping with blood . . . brandishing sabres, clubs, knives, axes." A panicky Arlette runs down the slope, and once catching sight of the tartane shrieks for help from Peyrol. Like "the incarnation of pale fury," she comes on board, fervently pleading with Peyrol to give Réal back to her. The entire scene is now excruciating as we behold Arlette in a fit of rage and desperation going faint and rigid in the arms of Peyrol. Danger and fatality seem to envelop the tartane, and a heavy, angry rain suddenly sweeps over the tartane, "as if this had been the beginning of a destroying and universal deluge—the end of all things." Suspense and mystery merge almost pitilessly as irreversible decisions are soon to be made that will affect forever the fates not only of Arlette and Réal but also of Peyrol, the loyal Michel, and Scevola. A buildup of momentum

[12]Moser, 179ff.

characterizes a certain inevitability in the events that will transpire, in this penultimate chapter (15), and that will reach a climax in the next and last chapter. Peyrol, at the epicenter of these events, is in complete command here, his decisions cannot be overruled, even as all those who surround him accede to his authority. His is an overarching presence in these last pages, as Conrad endows him with power over life and death.

Through his final and consequential actions, Peyrol speaks for life and love itself, in defiance of the forces of antilife. The struggling, agonizing voice of redemption is heard here with unflagging decisiveness. It is precisely the attenuated moment *The Rover* has been questing for, synthesizing everything that has happened in a line of life-progression. Thus, Peyrol has contrived to save Réal, and in turn Arlette, by having the lieutenant take her limp body ashore, to the safety of the farmhouse, while Peyrol himself remains with the tartane, in effect replacing Réal "on service." Peyrol chooses to remain completely true to himself, "to his old wandering self which had known no softness and no hesitation in the face of any risk offered by life." After seeing off Réal and Arlette to relative safety, Peyrol with the assistance of the ever-faithful Michel, who is aware only "of his own insignificant position at the tail of all mankind"—"I have only you, Maître Peyrol," he says, with "becoming gravity"—casts off the lines that hold the tartane to the shore, as the vessel shoots out into the cove and the sea "speckled with white caps." Réal, "running madly towards the cove," and expecting Peyrol to give up the tartane to him, finds to his amazement that "the little craft had been spirited away. . . . The old man had always meant to go himself!"

The hour is nigh for the tartane "to walk the seas . . . to traffic with the enemy." The English captain aboard the *Amelia* has become keenly aware that "there was a craft acting suspiciously." On board the tartane in the meanwhile, Peyrol himself is aware that the corvette "had marked him for her prey," as he seeks "to lead the Englishman a dance and keep up his character of a man anxious to avoid capture." In the final chapter of *The Rover*, the reader witnesses the thrilling movements of the tartane, which had the advantage of speed from the start and seemed to be slipping away from the *Amelia*, with Peyrol's clever seamanship and resourcefulness extracting from Captain Vincent grudging admiration. With darkness approaching, the English realize that time is of the essence if the tartane is to be captured and searched. Clearly Peyrol's deception of the English captain is fully succeeding, as the "moment" has finally come for the final confrontation between the two vessels.

Aboard the tartane, a groaning and terrified Scevola is holding on desperately from falling into the sea, his actions in sharp contrast to Michel's loyalty to Peyrol and to the mission of the tartane, now being relentlessly pursued by the enemy ship. The entire episode is dramatically detailed as the sea-chase is coming to a fatal climax, which Peyrol resignedly anticipates: " 'That ship,' he says to Michel, 'will be alongside of us in less than half an hour. As she comes up they will open on us with musketry.' " Which is exactly what takes place, as the *Amelia* closes on her chase of the tartane. "Everything he [Peyrol] had planned had come to pass." The description of Peyrol's dying moments are especially moving and in keeping with Conrad's compassionate tribute to the old sailor, who feared not death but failure. It is the death of a hero that we view at the end of the chase as the "tartane tumbled like a lifeless corpse amongst the seas," carrying on it, funereally, the fallen bodies of the loyal Michel, the hated Scevola, and the valiant Peyrol who, in the final breaths of his life "beheld in a flash the days of his manhood, of strength and adventure[,] smiled to his visions and died."

Indeed, a reader will not easily forget a defining luminous moment when, mortally wounded, Peyrol strives to catch a last glimpse on the afterdeck of Michel: "He tried to utter his name, but his throat refused him even a whisper." No textual detail better evokes the bond of fidelity that ties the two men together, in death as in life. Inscribed in this short sentence is the essence of Peyrol's character, his capacity for human connection and sympathy. Just these few words give us a wondrous peek into Peyrol's soul, in all of its transparency and nobility. It is, too, Peyrol's capacity for otherness, one that transcends the prison house of self-concern and that emerges from the moral depths of being, that is also heightened by Peyrol's internal thought (found in the same paragraph and immediately preceding the sentence already quoted) regarding the faith of his "camarade." "And Michel? Was he dead or dying, that man without friends whom his pity had refused to leave behind marooned on the earth without even a dog for company?" Conrad's predominant tone in these concluding pages is both reverential and meditative, subsuming "the swish of breaking seas," "the sound of the wind," "the wash of the waves," the acute drama of "a long chase."

The English take possession of the tartane, and quickly discover "a sailcloth package corded and sealed." Soon, too, Admiral Nelson's *Victory* makes its appearance and Captain Vincent presents himself on board, in order to hand over the "enemy dispatches." Lord Nelson, "the Commander in-Chief of his Majesty's ships in the Mediterranean," learns the details of the tartane's engagement with the *Amelia.* What Captain Vincent says about Peyrol's "courage and determination" has particular relevance to the Admiral, "choking and gasping," "very thin and worn out," as he proceeds to examine the papers taken from the tartane. Returning to the *Amelia*, and the quiet of his cabin, Captain Vincent reflects on the events that transpired, and it is Peyrol who dominates his thoughts. The decision is made, too, to sink the tartane, still being dragged by the *Amelia*, and to permit the three dead bodies to remain on the craft. The captain, almost in awe, remembers Peyrol's bravery: "His ship makes a very good coffin for a seaman, and those men deserve better than to be thrown overboard to roll on the waves."

For the English captain full honor and tribute must be paid to the old rover as the tartane is to be sunk by three successive shots from the port bow-run on the *Amelia*. Captain Vincent makes certain that the tartane will not go down without its "colours flying," and orders a French tricolor ensign to be placed on the tartane by bending the French ensign on the halliards and swaying the tartane's mainyard to the masthead. Aboard the *Amelia* reigns a "profound but not disapproving silence" as the orders are carried out for the sinking of the tartane. The description of the sinking is one fraught with respectfulness and solemnity; and the scene itself is couched in wonder and sacrosanctness as the tartane gives a "sudden dip, followed by a slow, unchecked dive." Here we have Conrad, as master of language, in full control of his creative powers, as he recreates an ending worth commemoration, with a feeling of sadness that does not surrender to what Henry James speaks of as "the grim view": "At last the tricolor flag alone remained visible for a tense and interminable moment, pathetic and lonely, in the centre of a brimful horizon." But Conrad does not conclude this scene without the recognition of tragic reality that not only surpasses a fleeting symbolism of eternal hope, but also rejects the siren calls of illusion. At last the tricolor flag itself disappears beneath "the blue level of the Mediterranean," as all hands on board the *Amelia* watch and their subdued murmurs die out: "All at once it vanished, like a flame blown upon, bringing to the beholders the sense of having been left face-to-face with an immense, suddenly created solitude."

The memory of Peyrol, however, does not cease when "the floating hearse" carries him to the bottom of the sea. His character and deeds are remembered by those whose lives he touched and shaped in mysterious but lasting ways. Thus Arlette's aunt, Catherine, "a magnificent old woman with upright carriage and an austere, brown, wrinkled face showing signs of past beauty," arranges with the priest in the church of Ste. Marie Majeure for memorial masses to pray for Jean Peyrol's soul. She no doubt wants to express her gratitude to him for what he has done for Arlette, whom she once bitterly saw "as a selected object of God's wrath." Catherine was no longer "uncertain of the future," now that, thanks to Peyrol's heroic sacrifices, Arlette was saved from Scevola and the infamy he represented, and eventually united in marriage with Lieutenant Réal, who was also saved by Peyrol on that momentous night from inevitable death in the tartane. Wounded at the Battle of Trafalgar, fought off Cape Trafalgar, Spain, October 21, 1805, and that ended with Admiral Lord Nelson's victory over French sea power, Réal had escaped capture and retired with the rank of Captaine de Frégate. He returned to Escampobar, to Arlette, and "to a quiet and retired life, obscure in a sense but not devoid of dignity." After discovering at the bottom of the well on the farm Peyrol's garment of sailcloth, lined with "gold pieces of various ages, coinages and nationalities," Réal and his wife gave it up to the Government, "as the hoard of a man who had died intestate with no discoverable relations." This episode was to recall to the couple "the uncertain name of Peyrol" with renewed feeling. "From that time they talked of him openly, as though he had come back to live again amongst them." It has been in fact approximately twelve years since Peyrol, for most of his life "a rover of the outer seas," has returned to the Port of Toulon as "a master of a prize taken off the Cape by Citoyen Renaud, commander-in-chief of the Republican Squadron in the Indian Seas."

Now, too, a mythic quality surrounds Peyrol's name, reinforced by the arrival on the farm of "the cripple of the Madrague" as he rides on the back of "a very diminutive donkey of a light gray colour with dark points." The reappearance of Peyrol's old friend and helper—"*C'est un homme ça* are words of appreciation that Peyrol often used whenever he talked of the crippled man"—now further heightens their recollections of Peyrol. Past and present coalesce quietly and harmoniously in the final paragraphs of *The Rover* as Peyrol is remembered by Monsieur and Madame Réal and by the visitor "with his soft eyes, long face, and his pained smile." " 'Ah, one could talk a long time of him,' said the cripple." John Lehmann's comment, "This end has the justice and power of a great poetic tragedy," has apt significance in any discussion of Peyrol's heroic virtues. What the old rover has done, beyond the terrors of "the red hand of the Revolution," beyond the horrid strife and the shadow of death, is to magnify "the sense of triumphant life."[13] For Peyrol, as for Conrad, the power of redemption and the power of reconciliation are so deeply interfused that they ultimately become one. *The Rover* is the visibilization of these two mighty powers both in their unity of ascent and in their moral affirmation.

If, as it is sometimes claimed, a distinct weariness can be detected in *The Rover*, it is hardly that of a world-weariness surrendering to an attitude of futility, or to an abject realization that nothing matters, nothing has meaning. Such a claim is the facile carryover of D. H. Lawrence's view, expressed in a letter dated October 30, 1912, condemning Conrad for "being so sad and giving in." *The Rover* rebuts this view with a vigor and a lucidity unusual for a writer very close to the end of a long career. There is no diminishment of artistic vision, nor of the values and principles that impelled and shaped Conrad's achievement. Continuity and consistency of vision distinguish this novel in highly concentrated ways, and with an exceptional economy of language aiming, above all, to communicate Conrad's creed of beliefs. It is his renewed sense of moral responsibility that is at the heart of *The Rover*, and that defines his central concerns and the way in which they are recreated in a measured story line. An elegiac note is distinctly heard here, but it is bathed neither in melancholy nor in sorrow. What we do hear is a comradely farewell; solemn and eloquent words anchored in equanimity and serenity; parting words in which Conrad is quietly speaking to the reader to keep in mind—to keep "the memory green," as he puts it—the virtues of loyalty and good courage that defy "the disenchantment that lurks in every day of a strenuous life" and that help one to steer carefully in a world which "seems to be mostly composed of riddles."[14] Called "the most finished"[15] of his novels, in the context of nobility of theme and purity of purpose, *The Rover* celebrates Conrad's passage from the tensions of spirit to the elevation of spirit.

---

[13]Morton Zabel, *The Portable Joseph Conrad*, rev. ed. (New York, 1969; 1947) 43.

[14]*The Mirror of the Sea* (New York, 1924; c1921) vii, ix.

[15]Jessie Conrad, *Joseph Conrad as I Knew Him* (London, 1926) 155.

Index